I0471414

BUILD & MARKET YOUR BUSINESS WITH GOOGLE

A Step-By-Step Guide to Unlocking the Power of Google and Maximizing Your Online Potential

by GabrielaTaylor

ISBN- 978-1490960777

Get FREE Content Marketing Plan Template
downloadable from my website:
www.gabrielataylor.com

Legal Notice

The publisher and author have strived to be as accurate and complete as possible in the creation of this book. The contents within are accurate and up to date at the time of writing however the publisher accepts that due to the rapidly changing nature of the Internet some information may not be fully up to date at the time of reading.

Whilst all attempts have been made to verify information provided in this publication, the Publisher assumes no responsibility for errors, omissions, or contrary interpretation of the subject matter herein. Any perceived slights of specific people or organizations are unintentional. This book makes no guarantees of success or implied promises. The strategies detailed in these pages will work, but are dependent on the work ethic and diligence of the reader.

All Rights Reserved

Dedicace

This book is dedicated to my parents and my brother. Eternal thanks for all your love and support. Without your encouragement I would not be able to do today what I've always dreamt of doing.

Thank you for everything you have ever given me.

TABLE OF CONTENTS

ABOUT THE AUTHOR

Gabriela Taylor (www.gabrielataylor.com) is an internationally educated Global Online Marketing Strategist and Consultant who's worked with some of the world's biggest brands in Telecommunications, Retail, Lifestyle and Advertising.

A recognized expert and specialist in Social Networking, Mobile Marketing and Search Engine Optimization, she is fluent in 7 languages, has lived and worked in many countries throughout the world and has experience of implementing successful web-presence strategies for both startup and large established organizations. She is fully certified in Google AdWords and Analytics and furthermore is an experienced coach and business mentor.

She is the founder of Global & Digital (www.globalndigital.com), a publishing company specializing in assisted self-publishing, marketing and mentoring for independent authors. Global & Digital specialise in helping published or first-time unpublished authors take their work to market in digital, print and audio formats. Gabriela is also actively involved in other businesses offering Online and Offline Marketing services, Cross-Cultural business consultancy and has published several industry related books:

- *Pinterest Marketing: The Ultimate Guide*
- *Socialize To Monetize: How to Run Effective Social Media Campaigns Across the Top 25 Social Networking Sites*
- *Building and Marketing Your Business with Google*
- *Zero Budget Marketing: How to Start & Market an Online Business with Little or Zero Marketing Budget*
- *Advertising in a Digital Age: Best Practices for AdWords and Social Media Advertising*
- *Globalize to Monetize: Taking Your Online Business to New Markets*
- *Plan, Create, Optimize, Distribute: Your Strategic Roadmap to Content Marketing Success*
- *Targeting Your Market: Marketing Across Generations, Cultures & Gender*
- *Mobilize to Monetize: The Fast Track to Effective Mobile Marketing*
- *Tumblr for Business: The Ultimate Guide*

Connect with the Author:

Website – www.gabrielataylor.com

Twitter – www.twitter.com/globalndigital

Pinterest – www.pinterest.com/taylorgabriela

Linkedin – www.linkedin.com/in/gabrielataylor

Facebook – www.facebook.com/globalndigital

INTRODUCTION

The average startup will fail within the first five years simply because there is either not enough time or not enough capital to allow it to remain functional. With limited cash flow and even more limited revenues coming in, profitability is ridiculously difficult to achieve. While technology makes it possible for anyone to start a business within minutes and promote it to everyone, everywhere, and at anytime, the competition is now stiffer than ever. As a small business owner with an online presence, you must use the power of the Internet to your advantage to not become another failed startup statistic. In particular, fully understanding the power of Google and what the vast array of Google tools can do for the growth of your business (when used knowledgeably) is essential. The vast majority of Google tools are free and it is difficult to overestimate just how effective they can be to drive the online success of your business.

Google is an intrinsic part of our daily online lives. It is the world's largest search engine by an immeasurable margin, is widely used for online email storage, as a map and navigation tool, is a rapidly growing social networking site and is the number one choice of the masses when searching for images and video content. There is no doubt that we have a massive reliance on Google for our entire online experience. There is also no question that Google is an incredibly successful organization that has transformed our online world, made huge amounts of money through its successful advertising strategy and is absolutely essential for any business that wants to make money online. Just how can you through, as a small business, make the most of the vast array of tools that Google has to offer?

This book unlocks the power of Google and how you can make this search giant work for you and your business. You will learn more about the full suite of Google tools, and how you can use them to launch and grow your business and have a successful online strategy by understanding exactly what you can get from Google and what Google can do for you. Google has over 100 apps and services that you can use for free. In this book I will cover off the key tools that you'll need and in particular I'll go through those tools that I personally use for my own business.

This book will guide you step-by-step through the process of setting up your online business to the point where startup and online presence converts to customers and sales. Everything you want, Google has. I will guide you through some of the basic business communication tools Google has to offer, and will discuss marketing your business with Google's social networking tools. I'll even talk you through using some of the more technical aspects of Google AdWords and Analytics. This book, I believe, is unique in that it not only takes a logical step-by-step approach to building your business with Google tools, but also covers each of these key tools in more detail than any other publication. I hope you enjoy my approach and get from this book exactly what you need to start maximizing the potential of your online business. Below I've listed the steps we'll cover:

Step 1: Set up for Success

Google's productivity tools are an efficient online solution for those businesses that want to stay organized and set up for success. While the perfect tools may be different for each one of us, depending on our specific needs, in my work I use daily productivity tools such as *Gmail, Calendar, Docs and Chrome.*

Step 2: Gather Internet Intelligence

Before starting an online business you need to gather Internet intelligence: search and research your industry, competition and competitors, and the best keywords for your site. And Google has the right tools for this as well: *Keyword Planner, Google Suggest, Related Searches, Google Display Network Ad Planner, Google Trends and Google Finance.*

Step 3: Establish an Online Presence

Once the research is done you can move on to establishing your online presence by building a user friendly website with *Blogger* or *Google Sites.* To facilitate navigation on the site and tell Google about your site pages create and submit a *Sitemap* to Google. *Google Shopping* and *Google Wallet* are also imperative for an ecommerce business.

Step 4: Understand the Power of SEO

After setting up your site, the next step is to optimize it in such a way that it becomes visible to your target audience. Most online businesses do not channel enough traffic to their site and fail to make sales because they have not made themselves visible to their customers. Nowadays, customers are presented with plenty of choices online. Thus, you need to find ways to draw their attention to your business and away from your competitors. Online optimization requires you to be proactive, creative and innovative. There is *on-site optimization* and there is *off-site optimization.* In addition you have the entire world at your disposal: *do you standardize or do you localize?* All of these will be discussed later in this book.

Step 5: Interact with Your Community

Now that you've done your research and you've built a website, it's time to interact with your community. Just putting an user friendly website online doesn't necessarily mean that you'll start getting customers. You need to let people know why you are different from your competition and learn how to gain their trust. *Google+*, *YouTube* and *Google News* are all tools that will help expand your online presence and facilitate interaction with your community.

Step 6: Grow Your Business with Paid Advertising

Earlier I said that most Google tools are free. However, for *Google AdWords* you will need to pay. This can be a very effective way to drive traffic to your site, but is by no means the only way. Google *AdWords* is a pay-per-click program using keywords, and represents the fastest way to bring traffic to your site. However, before you start using it, you need to know how to use it properly, otherwise you can lose a lot of money very fast.

Step 7: Monetize Your Content

If you have a lot of valuable content on your site and a lot of daily traffic you can start earning money by adding Google ads to your site. You pay for AdWords, but you are paid for *AdSense.* Some find this advertising model very confusing, but it's not. AdWords is like normal advertising, such as a flyer or an ad you take out in a newspaper (the ads will be placed across the web on either other sites, YouTube or on Google Search). On the other hand, *AdSense* is YOU owning the newspaper (your website) and others purchasing advertising space from you. They both work with targeted keywords.

Step 8: Feature on Daily Deals

You've probably heard of Groupon, the global deals company that Google tried to purchase last year for $6 billion. In response to Groupon's refusal to sell, Google bought DailyDeals.de in September 2011, a Groupon clone website based in Germany. *Google Offers,* launched in May 2011, is currently available only in the US (in more than 40 cities) and gives anyone with a product or service the opportunity to get new customers. So if you are a US based business, this is a great opportunity as a startup to get your product in front of customers. For businesses outside the US, *Google Offers* has plans to expand so watch this space.

Step 9: Monitor Brand, Competitors and Industry

As you progress with setting up and growing your business, you shouldn't forget to monitor your brand and keep an eye on what your competitors are doing and what's happening in your industry. *Google Alerts* is just what you need to make this possible.

Step 10: Track, Measure and Improve

No business can make decisions without tracking, measuring and improving. *Analytics* and *Webmaster Tools* were created to better understand your website and your site visitors, and react accordingly.

There are many more Google Products you can use to enhance your business on the Internet, but the ones I've mentioned above are the most recommended. Why pay for expensive tools when these Google tools already exist, provide you with everything you need and, with the exception of one or two of them, are available for free?

Chapter 1
A BRIEF HISTORY OF THE INTERNET

In 1993, two years before Sergey Brin and Larry Page (co-founders of Google) met, 15 million people in 50 countries were using the Internet, and just over 100 sites were already online. For a better understanding of Google, I suggest we take a look at the main events in the online world prior to – and after – Google's launch.

1957

USSR launches into orbit *Sputnik*, their first spacecraft satellite. In response to this, one year later USA creates ARPA (Advanced Research Projects Agency), responsible for researching ways to protect and transfer vital information in case of an attack in a nuclear war.

1969

Computers at the Universities of Stanford and UCLA are connected for the first time.

1970

Harvard, MIT and BBN are connected for the first time via the ARPA network.

1971

FTP and PROJECT GUTENBERG: Books and documents in the public domain are made available for free and in a variety of digital formats.

1973

The first trans-Atlantic connection is established between US and UK universities.

1974

B. Kahn and V. Cerf use the term INTERNET for the first time.

1975

The first modern email program with the addition of the REPLY and FORWARD functionalities is created.

1977

The first PC modem is introduced.

1978

The first unsolicited commercial email message called SPAM is born.

1979

MUD, the earliest form of multiplayer games, is designed (text based). MUD is precursor to World of Warcraft and Second Life.

USENET is launched, allowing people worldwide to communicate by posting messages in newsgroups.

M. Aldrich invents online shopping (at that time called "teleshopping").

1980

ENQUIRE, a hypertext program used by scientists to keep track of projects and people, is launched.

1982

France Telecom invents MINITEL, the most successful pre-worldwide online service.

The first emoticon ever used is :-). S. Fahlman suggests its use at the end of a written joke.

1984

Domain Name System (DNS) is introduced.

Cisco Systems (multinational that designs, manufactures and sells networking equipment) is founded.

1985

The WELL, called "the most influential online community in the world," is launched.

symbolics.com is the first .COM registered domain.

1987

The Internet grows to 30,000 hosts.

1988

IRC (Internet Relay Chat) allowing real time text messaging is launched.

The first malicious Internet attack called "The Morris Worm" is released.

1989

Tim Berners-Lee (British engineer and professor at MIT and also physicist at the CERN Laboratory) invents the Web with HTML as its publishing language. On the next page there is a screenshot of the first ever webpage.

AOL (America Online), a global Internet services company, is launched.

Peapod starts selling groceries online.

1990

The first commercial dial-up ISP is launched.

The World Wide Web opens up for commercial use as the WWW browser becomes available for download via FTP.

GOPHER, the first content-based search protocol, is launched.

The Internet Society is founded.

There are 26 web servers worldwide.

Network Solutions (domain registration business launched in 1979) begins registration services for .COM, .NET, .ORG and .GOV.

There are 200 web servers worldwide, 15 million Internet users and over 100 sites.

M. Andreessen creates the first web browser – called MOSAIC – with the aim of being used by the general public.

The first .ORG and .GOV domains are registered and they are for the **United Nations'** and the **White House's** websites.

MOSAIC changes its name to "Netscape Navigator."

Internet Search Engines such as **Yahoo**, Excite and Infoseek go live.

First bank to open online.

Pizza Hut starts to take online orders.

Match.com (online dating site) and **FedEx** (logistics company) are launched.

1995

The first SSL (Secure Sockets Layer) encryption, used to make online payments safer, is developed.

JavaScript is introduced.

Network Solutions starts charging for domain names. People are charged $100 for a two-year registration domain.

Internet Explorer 1.0 is launched.

More search engines are launched, including Go.com and AltaVista.

Echo Bay (later became eBay) and **Amazon.com** are launched.

Vatican goes online.

The number of Internet hosts reaches 4 million.

1996

Hotmail, the first webmail service, goes live.

Flash 1.0 is introduced.

Ticketmaster (ticket sales and distribution company) and **Shopzilla** (price comparison service) go online.

The number of Internet hosts reaches 9 million.

Steve Jobs returns to Apple.

Babel Fish (free text and web page translation company now owned by Yahoo), **Netflix** (provides TV shows and movies via the Internet), **GoDaddy** (Internet domain registrar) and **About.com** (provides online information and advice on various topics) are launched.

The number of Internet hosts reaches 16 million.

"Bill Clinton and Monica Lewinsky scandal" becomes the first story to be announced first online instead of through the traditional media.

The Microsoft Antitrust Trial begins.

Google, **PayPal** (acquired by eBay in 2002), **Napster** (peer-to-peer file sharing service) and **Alibaba Online** (Chinese investment holding company) are launched.

SETI@home project aiming to look for signs of extra-terrestrial intelligence is launched.

Baidu, the Chinese search engine, is launched.

Tencent QQ (Chinese instant messaging platform) is launched. The first English version of the site only goes live in 2009.

Zappos (bought by Amazon in 2009) launches a web-only shoe store.

Monster.com (worldwide job search platform) and **Blogger** (blog publishing service acquired by Google in 2003) go online.

The Domain **business.com**, purchased in 1997 for $149,000, is sold to eCompanies for US $7.5 million.

2000

The stock market crashes due to the dotcom bubble burst.

TripAdvisor (travel website) goes online.

2001

Amazon launches a mobile version of their site.

Wikipedia and **StumbleUpon** (discovery engine for photos, videos and web pages) go online.

2002

WordPress (free blogging tool), **Technorati** (blog search engine), **Last.fm** (online music catalogue), **TinyURL** (free

URL redirection service) and **SkyScanner** (flight search engine) go online.

Skype (acquired by eBay in 2005 and then by Microsoft in 2011) is launched.

MySpace (social networking), **Linkedin** (professional social networking), **Del.icio.us** (social bookmarking service, acquired by Yahoo in 2005), **SecondLife** (virtual world platform where users can socialize), **CouchSurfing** (network with free accommodation and advice for travelers) and **The Pirate Bay** (file sharing site) go online.

Apple launches **iTunes.**

Taobao (Chinese online action site) is launched by Alibaba.

CAN-SPAM Act states that it is illegal to send unsolicited emails.

The term "**Web 2.0**" is used for the first time in a Conference organized by Tim O'Reilly.

"The Facebook" opens to college students.

Other Social Media Networks such as **Digg** (social news site), **Reddit** (social news site), **Mixx** (helps users to share or find content based on interest and location) and **Flickr** (image and video hosting site) are launched.

Alipay (Chinese third-party online payment platform) is launched.

YouTube goes live.

Google Earth, **AdWords** and **Analytics** are launched.

Twitter is launched.

WikiLeaks (online organization that provides secret information from anonymous sources) and **Google Checkout** launched.

Google Street View, Tumblr (microblogging platform), **Experience Project** (social network that connects people through shared life experiences) and **Prestashop** (ecommerce platform that lets you build and maintain an online store) are launched.

Amazon launches the **Kindle** device.

The **iPhone** is also launched.

Web 3.0, also known as "semantic web" with the Internet of everything and everywhere, is born.

"Internet Election" – Obama takes full advantage of the Internet to promote himself. This is the first time that a candidate for any presidency uses the Internet for such purposes. He raises almost $200 million online.

Spotify (music streaming service), **Jinni** (movie search engine and movie recommendations that can be connected to a Netflix account), **Dropbox** (file hosting service) and **Groupon** (online deals website) are launched.

Bing, **Google Docs**, **Kickstarter** (worldwide funding platform for creative projects), **Web 2.0 Suicide Machine** (lets you remove friends/followers or content from various social networks), **Foursquare** (location-based social network) and **Quora** (questions and answers site) are launched.

The first non-Latin web addresses go live.

Pinterest (social photo sharing site), **Instagram** (an online photo-sharing, video-sharing and social networking service) and **Magento Mobile** (ecommerce platform) are launched.

Klout (social media analytics site) goes live.

Google+ is launched.

Steve Jobs dies.

Google Drive is launched.

634 million websites are online.

There are 1.1 billion global smartphone subscribers.

Instagram is acquired by Facebook for $1 billion.

Twitter acquires **Vine** (create and post 6seconds video clips).

There are 2.4BN Internet users worldwide (source: internetworldstats.com).

YouTube announces 1 billion monthly users.

If you'd like more details on the history of the Internet and technological revolution, I'd recommend checking out:

- Isaac Asimov predicted the Internet of today 20 years ago - bit.ly/isaacasimov

- "The Virtual Revolution", a documentary from BBC that shows how the Web transformed our lives.

- "Nerds 2.0.1: A Brief History of the Internet" by Mark Stephens is a three-hour documentary broadcasted in 1998 - bit.ly/nerdsvideo

- "A brief history of the Internet" by Philip Roenthal explains the evolution of the Internet from a 1957 government experiment to the advent of web-enabled "smartphones" 50 years later - bit.ly/philiprosenthal

- "History of the Internet" by Melih Bilgil presents in an animated documentary the Internet inventions, from time-sharing to filesharing - bit.ly/melihbilgil

Chapter 2
GOOGLE AT A GLANCE

Most people know the basic history of Google – how Larry Page and Sergei Brin met while at Stanford University and created a program that would return results for a keyword searched. Initially known as "BackRub" and soon re-named "Google" after the mathematical term "Googol," their program became popular thanks to the PageRank algorithm that ranks a page by the number of links it receives from other pages.

Both Larry and Sergey had a big passion for technology from childhood, and very similar upbringings. They were both born in 1973, their fathers were college professors and both of their mothers were scientists. They both attended Montessori elementary schools (individual learning with little input from the teachers and focus on personal development).

The culture they brought and maintained at Google is a startup culture, where people are the main resource and where abilities are more appreciated than experience. At Google, people are encouraged to work 20% of their work time on personal projects that could make a difference to the world.

Google.com was registered in 1997 and now has more than 100 products and services, of which Search, YouTube and Gmail are the most used. Google didn't launch anything new, but improved already existing products in the market, and this attracted a lot of criticism (including copywriting, censorship, privacy and rank manipulation). Along the way they also faced several challenges from their competitors: Yahoo (product AdWords), Viacom (product YouTube), Rupert Murdoch and other big publishers (product Google News), Verizon (Google Mobile), etc.

"Once you get to a certain size, you have to figure out new ways of growing. And then you start leaking on everyone else's industry. And when you do that, you sort of wake up the bears, and the bears come out of the woods and start beating the shit out of you," says Ivan Seidenberg, CEO of Verizon.

From 1998 to today, Google has grown into the largest search engine in the world (see graphic on the next page). They started with 10,000 queries a day, and one year later were serving over 500,000 queries a day. Now they are getting more than a billion per day, and more than half of these come from outside the US (source: Google Internal Data).

The year 2000 was a turning point for Google. They announced their ability to read minds as they created MentalPlex, the April Fools' Day hoax that is still eagerly awaited each April 1st. Google was released in several languages: French, German, Swedish, Finnish, Spanish, Portuguese, Dutch, Norwegian, Danish and Italian, followed a few months later by Chinese, Japanese and Korean. In 2000, Google won their first "Webby Award" for technical achievement, as voted by users. They also became the Yahoo! default search provider and were the first to have one billion URLs indexed in their database. This made them the world's largest search engine.

From then until today, it's all been uphill, with small molehill snags along the way. After Google started their search engine, they looked around for ways to make money with it. They came up with **Google AdWords**, which became the world's leading online advertiser. Initially AdWords only had 350 customers – now it brings in 75% of the Google's total revenue. The **Google Toolbar** was also launched in 2000.

2001

In February 2001, Google made their first acquisition of Deja Usenet, which was later integrated with Google Groups. By that time, Usenet had about 500 million discussions. In July 2001, Google launched Google Images, with 250 million images indexed. By December 2011 they had over 3 billion web pages indexed. Eric Schmidt was hired as CEO and Larry was appointed President of Products, and Sergey as President of Technology. Only three years old, the search engine was already available in 26 languages, and opened its first international office in Tokyo.

2002

In 2002, Google partnered with AOL to become its default search provider. In May, they opened Google Labs, a beta technology from the research and development team. It allowed users to try out various Google tools before they were released to the masses. If they didn't work out, they were discontinued. This useful product was shut down in 2011. 2002 was also the year when Google launched **Google News –** with 4000 news sources – and Froogle – later renamed **Google Product Search**. During the same year, Google opened their second international office in Australia and made their search engine available in 72 languages.

In 2003, linguists recognized the word "Google" as the most useful word of 2002. Google acquired Prya Labs (owner of **Blogger**, a free blog platform still in use today) and Applied Semantics (a technology that augments **AdSense**). They also launched Google Grants, Google Print (later renamed **Google Book Search**) and content-targeted advertising service for AdWords.

In February 2004, Google claimed to have 8 billion web pages indexed, which included 880 million images. New companies were acquired, including Keyhole (later the basis for Google Earth and Google Maps), **Orkut** and **Picasa**. They also went public with an IPO at $85 per share. With more than 3000 employees, Google opened their first European office (in Dublin, Ireland), their first office in Greater China (based in Hong Kong) and two offices in Bangalore and Hyderabad, India. Several products were launched in 2004: **Google SMS**, **Gmail, Google Desktop** and the first **Official Google Blog.** They also launched **Google Scholar** and entered into a partnership with Harvard, Stanford, University of Michigan and Oxford, as well as the New York Public Library, to scan books into Google Book Search.

During this year they launched **Google Code**, **Google Analytics** (after Urchin was acquired), **Google Blog Search**, **Google Reader**, **Google Earth, Google Maps** and several mobile related products. They acquired **Android** and opened the first Latin America offices in São Paulo and Mexico City.

Google acquired **YouTube**, JotSpot (which was used to build **Google Sites**), dMarc (a digital radio advertising company) and Writely (which became the basis for **Google Docs**). Several new products were introduced, such as **Picasa**, **Chat in Gmail**, **Google Trends**, Google Checkout (later renamed **Google Wallet**), **Google Customer Search, Finance** and **Calendar**. "Google" was added as a verb in the Oxford English Dictionary. The Queen of England launched the Royal Channel, which made her the first monarch to have an Internet presence. Google.cn went live.

Google introduced **Universal Search**, a search engine that incorporates all kinds of searches: text, video, images, etc. Zeitgeist was replaced by **Hot Trends**. Street View in Google Maps went live and Google Maps was introduced on the iPhone. New companies were acquired, two of them being AdScape (an in-game advertising company) and reCAPTCHA (which digitizes the text of books while protecting sites from bots intrusion).

2008

Google acquired **DoubleClick**, an Internet advertising company that is used to serve up ads based on your previous searches and follow your surfing habits by leaving markers on your computer (called cookies). Google's own browser, called **Google Chrome,** was launched. Google Earth became available to iPhone and iPod, and **creative commons on Google Image Search** was introduced. Street view for Google Maps was almost completed within the United States. New products such as **Google Suggest, Website Optimizer** and the first **Android powered phone** were launched. Magazines were added in Book Search, and a new partnership with Yahoo was established.

2009

Google created their own Twitter account and tweeted the following message *"I'm 01100110 01100101 01100101 01101100 01101001 01101110 01100111 00100000 01101100 01110101 01100011 01101011 01111001 00001010."* Ten new languages were added to **Google**

Translate. The Vatican opened its own YouTube channel, and the White House had a town hall question/answer time on **Google Moderator**. Admob, a mobile advertising platform, was acquired.

2010

Picnik, a photo-sharing platform, was acquired. This is now integrated with Google+.

2011

Google+ was launched.

Zagat, a restaurant ratings and review company, was acquired by Google.

2012

A new SEO algorithm called "Google Penguin" was released. **Google+ Local** replaced Google Maps and **Google Shopping** replaced Google Product Search. Google was censored in China. Senior roles within Google are changed. Larry Page replaces Eric Schmidt as CEO, Sergey Brin gets involved in strategic projects and new products and Eric Schmidt starts *"focusing externally on deals, partnerships, customers and broader business relationships, government outreach and technology thought leadership"*. **Google Drive** and **Knowledge Graph** were launched.

Google Glasses were released. **Google Reader** was shutdown. Google Shopping had completed transition to a commercial model in several European countries, Brazil, Australia and Japan. Google Keyword Tool was replaced by **Google Keyword Planner**.

For more details on the Google's history, check out: google.com/about/company/history

That's all for now on the history of the Internet and Google. That gives you a whistle-stop tour of how the Internet and Google got to where they are today. It is very important to understand and acknowledge where Google has come from in order to fully appreciate what its array of tools can do for you and your business today. Let's now take a look at some of the tools I recommend you use for your business.

Chapter 3
SETTING UP FOR SUCCESS: PRODUCTIVITY TOOLS THAT YOUR STARTUP OUGHT TO USE

Did you know that Google productivity tools could save a business that employs just four people over $32,000 per year?

From e-mail to instant editing and planning solutions, Google can save your startup a ton of liquidity so that you can do more with the limited resources you have. It doesn't matter if you are the only person in the startup or if you've got a handful of employees – you can save time, money and resources by utilizing Google's productivity tools today for your new venture.

The Google's productivity tools that I'll be discussing in this chapter are **Google Apps, Chrome and iGoogle.**

Google Apps is web-based software that allows you to collaborate with other users, simply by being "in the cloud" (or connected to the Internet). This means that you, your employees and your clients can access documents, discuss meetings, schedule events and work on projects from anywhere in the world. All you need is a reliable Internet connection, as Google guarantees that 99% of the time their servers will be functioning to full capacity. After all, when one part of the world is sleeping, another part of the world is just starting their day. If you are trying to make your startup play on a global level, you've got to be available all the time.

Google has a free offering of its online Apps. This suite allows for up to 10 users and comes with features such as Gmail, Calendar, Drive, Docs, Sites, Vault and more. The free version is suitable for individuals and small businesses that are just starting up and do not have large business communication and collaboration needs. The paid Google Applications have similar features to the unpaid suite, but the paid versions offer greater storage space and allow more user interaction. As your business grows, it would be a good idea to upgrade to Google Business Apps. This will allow greater flexibility and reliability in your business communication needs.

Without even covering the other aspects of the Google productivity tools – such as video meetings, instant messaging and over the web chatting (which can allow business partners in several different locations to work together efficiently) – you've already saved over $40K per year in operating costs and man hours by going with Google instead of the traditional IT solutions. Over a five-year period, that's over $200K worth of operating costs that you have eliminated. What could your startup do with $200K of fresh cash liquidity that has been freed up through increased employee production and fewer expenses?

It is time now to look at the Google productivity tools and understand how you can make better use of them in your business.

Gmail

Gmail is Google's online email service. It is a "cloud" web service, meaning that it stores all your data and emails online. As such, you are able to access your emails from any computer or phone, irrespective of your geographical location. Additionally, Gmail gives you access to email even without an Internet connection. Initially, Gmail was largely used by individuals as a personal email service. However, this web service offers significant benefits and features for businesses too. Gmail is a free service with features that make it a versatile interface to communicate and collaborate with employees and clients. You can also search through your emails with Gmail and store the ones you want to save without worrying if they will be deleted or not. Google gives you 10 years to decide if you want to delete them or not.

There are in-built features on Gmail that you can use to customize your Gmail interface to your specific business demands.

Create a Gmail Account on Your Own Domain - Gmail, as a feature of Google Apps, allows you and your business to look professional by creating a Gmail account that includes your company domain name. Instead of sending emails to clients with your "@gmail.com" address, you can incorporate your company's domain name so that your email reads "address@yourcompanyname.com." All of your employees can also get Gmail addresses with a similar format. This approach provides credibility to your business, as well as a brand identity that clients can identify with.

Customized Signature - Customizing a signature will save you the task of writing your name, title and contact details every time you send an email. In addition, a customized signature that includes informative snippets about your company serves as a subtle but effective marketing tool. To create a customized signature, use the "Settings tab" above your inbox and then insert your text signature.

Task Management - The task management tool in Gmail lets you integrate your to-do list on the email interface. With the task manager, you can create more than one to-do list, add reminders, add emails that you need to reply to, cancel tasks that you have completed and prioritize the tasks on your to-do list. The Task Manager is a component of Google Labs. Thus, you will need to go to Gmail Labs tab to activate the task manager tool. After enabling the Tasks icon, refresh the Gmail page to access the Task Manager tool.

Gmail Offline - Gmail allows you to access emails and to keep in contact with employees and clients even when you do not have an Internet connection. When you activate this tool through the Settings Tab, Gmail begins to store data into your computer's hard disk. This data is synchronized with Gmail servers so that when you go online, Gmail uses the data in its servers instead of relying on the Internet connection. The messages that you send while you are offline are stored in the Outbox and are sent as soon as Gmail detects Internet connectivity.

Send Automatic Replies - The "send automatic replies" function helps you save time when replying to familiar queries. You can access the "Canned Messages" tool from "Gmail Labs." Then, insert the messages, reports and replies that you commonly send to employees and clients, and save these. Every time you need to answer a common question, just click the "Canned Messages" link and choose the message you would like to send.

Send Email from Another Address - Gmail allows you to use addresses other than your current Gmail address to send and reply to emails. This allows you to manage emails from other accounts in a single Gmail interface. Visit the "Accounts and Import" option under the Gmail Settings Tab to activate this feature. To use an alternative sender address, click on "Add another email address you own."

Managing Different Email Accounts - Managing emails sent to different accounts is challenging and time consuming if you have to keep switching between different web services. Gmail lets you route up to five email accounts into the Gmail interface. Click on "Add a POP3 mail account you own" to add new email accounts. This option will redirect all the emails from your other accounts into your Gmail account, allowing you access to everything within a single interface.

Filter Spam from Your Email Account - Spam messages are unwanted messages that can clutter up your inbox. When spam messages get to your inbox, it can be difficult to differentiate between wanted and unwanted messages. To avoid wasting time on reading and deleting spam messages, Gmail filters these types of messages and keeps them from appearing in your inbox. If Gmail sends a message to the spam box that should be in your inbox, you can transfer this message to where it belongs. Through the new tool "Hub of Spam," Gmail allows you to determine the reasons why some messages were sent to the spam box.

Back up Your Gmail to Your Hard Disk - In the event that Google has a massive breakdown with its Gmail servers, it is possible, although highly unlikely, that you'll lose all the data stored in your Gmail account. The loss of essential data could be disastrous for your company. However, Gmail lets you save your emails and data onto your computer's hard disk. You can use the "Mozilla Thunderbird" email software to save your data. Visit the Settings Tab on the Gmail interface and choose the "Forwarding and POP/IMAP" option. Choose "POP," as it is simpler to use than IMAP. Then choose the "Enable POP for all mail" option. Then, select the option "Keep Gmail's Copy in the Inbox" because you are only backing up the data. Thunderbird will launch and request you to insert your Gmail username and password to allow this software to begin saving your emails and data.

Chat and Video Chat - Gmail chat allows you to communicate with employees and clients regardless of their location. The chat function lets you have an instant conversation, which takes a conveniently shorter delivery period of time than email. You can also host or attend videoconferences with clients and virtual employees through Video Chat. Alternatively, you can use voice messaging to communicate. You and the people you are communicating with only need to have a web camera and an activated video plug-in to hold video conversations.

Use Google Talk to Leave a Voice Message - Google Talk, a feature of Gmail, allows you to talk to your contacts for free, as long as Internet connectivity is available. The voicemail service lets you leave messages for clients when they are not available to talk with you at that moment. You can leave messages whether or not they are signed in to Google Talk. The voicemail service allows you up to ten minutes of talking time. Your clients or employee will be able to receive the voicemails you leave for them through their email accounts.

Share Media with Google Talk - If you are holding an IM (instant messaging) conversation through Google Talk and need to send a file or a video link, using the chat window, select "Send File Option" and then the file(s) that you want to send. You can either send files saved on your computer or send Internet links. The reception is instant and keeps the conversation flowing.

Apply Different Themes - You can create a customized Gmail interface that reflects your preferences and makes using Gmail much easier for you. Gmail's theme builder lets you choose theme colors and images that will then appear in the background of your interface. Once you apply the themes, they come on immediately. You can easily change them whenever you want. To create a customized Gmail inbox, visit the "Settings" tab on the interface and chose the "Themes" option.

Stop Sent Messages from Being Delivered - The new Gmail Lab feature "Got the Wrong Bob" enables you to stop your email's recipient from receiving a message. This feature is especially useful if you sent the wrong information to your client or employees. Activate this feature under the Lab tab in Settings. Gmail identifies the added or omitted recipient in a group email and then terminates the message before it reaches the recipient. "Don't Forget Bob" is another feature that suggests recipients that you might want to add when you send a new email. This feature ensures that you do not leave out any relevant clients or employees for whom the email is also meant.

Integrated Gmail - This is a Firefox add-on that simplifies your experience on Gmail. This add-on allows you to collapse the inbox so that you can add other gadgets that you are currently working on, or those gadgets that you use frequently. By collapsing the inbox, you are able to customize your interface by adding Google Apps, News Feeds, Calendar and Picasa. Integrated Gmail saves you the time that you would spend switching between tabs while using all these gadgets.

Google Mail Checker Plus - This is a Gmail add-on that allows you to manage your emails better. Available from "Gmail Lab," this feature enables you to read your email without leaving the tab that you are currently on, loading and re-loading Gmail whenever you want to check for new messages. By installing this ad-on, Gmail will send you updates on your computer about your inbox activity. You can also delete, filter spam, save and star the mail coming into your inbox. Mail Checker Plus will monitor this and send you the relevant notifications even if you are working on something else.

Gmail Drive - As a Gmail add-on, "Gmail Drive" acts as a virtual storage facility for your Gmail interface. It enables you to store files in the same way you would store them in your actual computer hard disk drive. This add-on allows you to utilize the Gmail interface as a storage space. Gmail Drive creates a new drive in the "My Computer" folder allowing you to save and access files from your Gmail from any browser that you are in. It allows you to create folders and files in the same way that you would on a hard drive.

Hide Gmail Ads - Gmail allows you to hide any advertisements that appear on the interface. These ads can be distractive, but you can remove them by visiting the Settings Tab and clicking on the "Web Clips," and then unchecking the "Show My Web Clips" above the inbox options. Hiding Gmail Ads that appear on your interface not only eliminates distraction but also gives you a wide looking interface for ease of use.

Boomerang for Gmail - This feature allows you to write emails that will be automatically sent on a later date. This feature is a Gmail add-on that helps you organize your business activities and appointments in a way that you will not leave out important tasks such as sending emails to your clients. You can also use Boomerang to avoid distraction from incoming emails. By activating this feature, you are able to divert emails from your inbox into another folder until you are ready to read them. In addition to keeping off distracting emails, this feature can also help you to un-clutter your inbox. Boomerang also alerts you when someone does not reply to your email.

Primary-Social-Promotions - You've probably discovered the new Gmail look where emails are automatically sorted in three inboxes: Primary, Social and Promotions. If you want your customers to receive your emails in their "Primary" inbox then advise them to un-check the "Promotions" box. If a mailing goes to more than just a few people, Gmail consider it as a promotion.

Google Calendar

Whether your business has one employee or more, organizing schedules, meetings and milestones can be a demanding task. Google Calendar, a feature in the Google Apps, offers an effective way of managing schedules and events, and synchronizing them across all users. Google

Calendar is a dynamic tool that allows you to utilize its different features, depending on the needs and nature of your business.

Create Schedules - One way of using Google Calendars to meet your business needs is to create calendars that are easily accessible by employees and your clients. You can make these types of calendars only accessible to specific employees and clients, who can then view the schedules and appointments you have with them. You can also add your employees and clients' calendar to your own to enable easier collaboration.

Color Coded Calendars - Google Calendar allows you to create multiple color-coded calendars that inform users of pending or upcoming appointments. In the event that appointments or schedules change, the color-coded calendar updates itself automatically, allowing users to remain up to date with these changes. Missing an appointment with a potential customer can negatively affect your business. When employees miss project deadlines, business productivity is compromised. With multi-color coded calendars, you, the clients and employees are able to know when deadlines and meetings are due and the actions to take.

Add Events - All users who have access to Google Calendar (gCalendar) through your domain are able to add events as they come up. For example, instead of sending out emails to employees and clients about an upcoming event or appointment, all you have to do is include this event in the Google Calendar interface. Both employees and clients who have access to this interface are then able to see the event and plan accordingly.

Synchronizing Your Schedules and Tasks - Small businesses that have just begun using Google Apps for business can synchronize their existing calendars in Microsoft Outlook with Google Calendar. Synchronizing Outlook calendars with Google Calendar allows you to continue using Outlook calendars anywhere. This is especially helpful if you or your employees find it easier to use the Outlook interface. It is also possible to synchronize mobile phone calendars with Google Calendars. This allows you to move easily between clients' contacts and appointments stored in your smartphone and those that are in your Google Calendar.

Event Notification - Google Calendar allows users to receive event notifications through email, multiple pop-ups and SMS. Users are able to receive notifications when events are added, schedules change or upcoming events are almost due. To receive notifications on the go, users have to register their phone number in Google Calendar. What this means for business is that communication between employer, employees and clients continues to be smooth and effective.

Invite Guests - Small businesses whose core functions include event organization can effectively use Google Calendar to invite guests to events. Guests, colleagues and friends who have access to your Calendar can receive invites, post responses and confirm their availability. This tool also allows you to coordinate these responses in an orderly manner.

Retrieve Reading Material - Google Calendar offers a reliable method of storing and retrieving any reading materials that you may have read in the past. Instead of looking through endless pages to find an article you can simply use Google Calendar. When you include a reading item in Pocket, Calendar will save the item's title as well as a link to the article as an event on the calendar. You can easily retrieve the item from Google Calendar simply by looking up a title or even a word in the title of the item you saved. You can also distribute your calendar to your contacts giving them the ability to see what you are reading and you can also share articles with them.

Facebook Posts Scheduled - If you host a Facebook page for an event or you are looking to publish the same type of post for a period of time, you can use Google Calendar to schedule posts to be published on Facebook. Google Calendar cannot differentiate between an actual event and a post marked as an event. You can include the day and specific time that you want the post to be published however this will only work if your calendar is public.

Managing Projects - Use Google Calendar to distribute tasks to team members and to display pending projects as well as upcoming deadlines. You can track the progress of these tasks using cues that are familiar to all of the team members.

Google Docs

Google Docs is a free suite of products that provide you with the tools to create and develop documents online, to work with others on the documents, to share these documents and to store them online. Through this application, you can access and work on word documents, spreadsheets, presentations, drawings and forms. Google Docs is a "cloud" suite, meaning that you can access your documents and continue with other tasks irrespective of your location or which computer you are using. You can also access documents when there is no Internet connection. To access Google Docs, you will require a Google Account. Use your Gmail username and password to sign in at docs.google.com.

As a small business, there are several ways that you can use the vast resources offered by Google Docs to bring efficiency and enhance collaboration in your business.

Share Documents - Sharing in Google Docs involves working on documents, spreadsheets, presentations and drawings with your team, clients or business associates. This is especially useful when different members of the team are located in different geographical locations. Up to 50 people can edit a document in real time, and when changes are made to the document, everyone is able to see this and respond appropriately. You no longer have to send documents as attachments through emails. You can keep your documents private, choose a select group of people to share with or publish them on the Web for the public to access. To share your documents, select the "Share" button at the right corner of the Google Docs interface, and then choose the visibility option that allows you to share the document with others. Include or remove those who can see and/or edit your documents. The people with whom you choose to share the document will receive a URL in their email with which they can access the shared documents.

Visibility Options - They are the levels of access you want your documents to have. As a business, there are documents you want to keep private. Others can be shared with employees and specific clients, while still others can be accessed by the greater public. The default visibility option is usually private, but you can change this according to your needs. "Anyone with a Link" is a visibility option that allows selected people with access to a document to view the document. By sending a URL link to employees or clients, they can easily access and collaborate with you on a document. To allow this visibility option, select the "Share" Tab on the left-hand panel of your interface, select "Change" and choose the "Anyone with a Link" option. Add the people who will have access to the document, paste the URL and then send it. Choose the "Public on the Web Option" if you want anyone to access it through search engines. Whoever has full access to the document can also edit it without your permission, so it's worth being careful with the access rights that you grant!

Upload or Export Documents - Google Docs allows you to upload and export pre-existing documents into your Documents List. This means that you can integrate the documents that were saved in your computer and store them in the Document List on the Google Docs interface. This way, you can access your documents and share them easily even when you are on the go. You can do this by dragging and dropping files from the "My Computer" folder on your PC, and dropping them into the Docs List. An easier method would be to visit the "Settings" Tab on the Google Docs interface, click on the "Upload" tab and then from the dropdown menu select the files you want to export or upload onto the Document Listing. When uploading several files at the same time, use the "shift" or "ctrl" tabs and click to enable uploading of all the files.

Revision History - Through Google Docs you can preview the changes that were made to a document, the time these changes were made and which team member made these changes. This is especially helpful in project management, as it allows you to keep track of who is doing what. Through the revision history panel, you can also see the previous version of the document and compare this to the changes made by collaborators. You can continue to edit the current version from where other collaborators left it, without deleting any of the previous versions of the document. To see the revision history, select the "File tab" on the Google Docs interface, and then "See Revision History." On the right-hand pane select "Time Duration" to see earlier versions of the document and the collaborators involved.

HTML View of Your Documents - A HTML view of your documents allows you to present your documents as a single presentation instead of demonstrating them in individual slides. Presenting your documents in the HTML version instead of the presentation view allows members of your team or clients who have screen readers to still access the documents easily. To present your document in HTML fashion, visit the "View menu" to the left on the Google Docs interface, and then choose the "HTML view."

Using the Chat Box - As you collaborate with your team or associates on documents, you can continue to have conversations concerning the project at hand. The Chat Box feature comes up automatically every time you and others come together to work on a document. The Chat Box shows the names of each collaborator, allowing you to communicate with them simultaneously, using this instant messenger feature as collaboration on the document is ongoing. To send a chat message to any of the collaborators, click on the arrow located on the right side of their name and open a tab to begin communicating.

Making Use of Templates - The templates available in Google Docs make it easy for you to create documents for the different tasks that you want to accomplish. The templates are particularly useful in the creation of schedules, resumes and application letters, invoices and catalogs. You can sort templates by popularity, category and type of document. To access the Template, select the Create button from your Documents List and then click on the "Template" tab to select the template that you would like to use. You may share these templates with others or keep them private.

Organizing Files - Google Docs allows you to store and access up to 5,000 documents in your Documents List. For easy retrieval of these documents and better organization, you can create Collections within which files are stored. Creating Collections is an excellent way of easily sharing multiple files with your team. Collections act as both folders and labels. You can store these collections in a hierarchical order and share them with your business team. To create a collection, click on the "Create tab" on the left-hand side of your Document List. Use the dropdown list and chose "Collection," then go ahead and name the Collection. The created Collection will appear in your Documents List and in the "My Collections" area on the left side of your interface. Generally, files are stored in one Collection, but you can place a file in as many Collections as suits your needs. Add a file to a Collection by dragging them from your Documents list and dropping them into the Collection. To better identify the Collections, you may apply different colors to each.

Working Offline - Google Docs allows you to safely access these documents when you do not have an Internet connection. This is especially helpful when you are traveling, as you can still carry out some tasks such as viewing documents and keeping up with the changes made by other team members. However, you cannot edit documents offline. To access Google Docs offline you must first activate the feature on your computer and from any computer you are likely to use. Simply go to your "Documents List" and select the offline mode. Be sure to activate "offline mode on personal computers only," otherwise anyone can access your documents.

Google Cloud Connect - Google Cloud Connect is an add-on for Microsoft Office suite. This add-on allows you to collaborate and share Microsoft Word, PowerPoint and Excel documents with your team members. This plug-in syncs Microsoft documents with the Google Docs interface. Each document that you synchronize is allocated a URL address that you can share with your team members or clients via email or Instant Messenger (IM). Follow the same procedure of sharing documents to add the people with whom you want to collaborate on a document.

Translation - To make documents accessible to clients or associates of different nationalities, you may use the translation feature. There are 53 languages available in Google Docs. Visit the 'Tools" menu at the top of your interface, choose the "Translate Documents" option and then click on the language you would like to translate the document into. A machine translation will not be as accurate as a human translation, but they are becoming more and more accurate and can facilitate communication in an emergency.

Dropdown Lists on Spreadsheets - They save you a lot of time when working on categories and subcategories. Instead of manually entering data and ranges into each cell, you can create dropdown lists that can do this task for you. Entering name ranges makes the various formulas you use simpler.

Through Google Docs, you may create dropdown lists by validation against a pre-existing range, or from a custom list that you create on your own to reflect your specific need.

Data Validation - Google Docs provides you with the tools to validate the inputs made by other people who are collaborating on a spreadsheet. Data Validation enables you to control the numbers, dates and texts inserted. By using this feature, you are able to maintain a spreadsheet with correct details.

Embedding: To make your document public, you can embed it within a blog or website. First, publish the document by going to the "Share Menu" on the right corner of the page and click on the "Publish as a Webpage" Option. If you wish to publish sections of your document, choose which ones and then select the "Publish Now" tab. Google Docs will create a URL for your document, which you can then use to embed on a webpage.

Speaker Notes on a Presentation - When making a presentation – for example, a sales presentation to your clients – use the speaker notes to help you remember important points. Visit the "View" menu on the interface and choose the "Show Speaker Notes" option. A window will appear in which you can add and display the notes that will accompany the presentation slides.

Creating Google Drawings - Google Drawings enables you to create and collaborate on company flow charts, design diagrams, pie charts and other visual/graphic representations. This feature also lets you communicate with other collaborators via a chat box. Additionally, you may publish and embed or even upload images from your computer for use on the Google Drawings interface.

Using Google Forms - Google forms will come in handy when you are conducting surveys for your products or services, collecting information from employees and customers, or when conducting interviews. Google forms are, by default, synchronized with spreadsheets that have the same title as the form. This helps you to tabulate results in spreadsheets using the information you receive from the form. To get started with Forms, go to the "New Forms" in your Documents List and choose a theme. The responses that are generated from the forms will appear in a spreadsheet tab that is accessible to you at any time. It is possible to share documents with your customers or team members via email or the social network Google+.

Google Chrome

Google Chrome is Google's primary web browser that was launched in 2008 and now has more than 200 million users, making it the most popular browser worldwide, ahead of Internet Explorer and Mozilla Firefox. Google Chrome is a feature that allows you to carry out online tasks such as accessing mail, searching for information, reading news and interacting in social networking sites. As a business, using a browser that is fast, easy to use, versatile and efficient is important. More and more businesses are choosing to use the Google Chrome browser due to the diverse features that it offers its users. Below I have listed several ways that you can make this browser work for your business.

Using the Search Bar - The search bar, one of Chrome's prominent features, allows you to find information easily. It only requires you to type in a keyword or a website's URL, and information about this word or URL is generated. As you spend your time online, you might need to open numerous tabs at the same time to aid you with your searches. With Google Chrome, you can open as many tabs as you need. You may easily navigate from one tab to another while in the same window. Google's browser has designed its search features in a way that allows you to close only the non-responsive tabs, and not the entire window.

Using the Task Bar - Google Chrome provides you with an easy to use interface that allows you to easily navigate the browser. From Chrome's task bar, you can access email, documents, calendars, documents, translation, latest news and images, and have quick access to social networking sites. The task bar is designed in such a way that it will save you a lot of time, as it enables you to access information fast. Chrome's easy to use interface also allows you to manage your browsing history. The browser stores pages visited in the last 10 weeks. This means that you can conveniently retrieve information that you have viewed in the past without needing to look up this information from a search engine again.

Bookmarking - Bookmarking sites that are important for your business goes a long way to saving time and storing information in an organized way. Chrome allows you to manage and create as many bookmarks as you need. Additionally, all bookmarks that are updated from one device will automatically be updated in another device. As a Chrome user, this allows you to "carry" your bookmarked web pages everywhere you go. In addition to these features, Google Chrome hosts a number of add-ons or extensions to enable both basic and advanced users to manage their online businesses and marketing strategies.

TOP 10 GOOGLE CHROME ADD-ONS

1. Screen Capture

Screen Capture allows users to capture and save screenshots of websites, images and videos that might be of interest. If you are making a presentation to a customer, screenshots can be used to make the presentation more vivid. You can make notes and edit the screenshots to your liking. Screen Capture provides you with the tools to create effective video marketing presentations of your own website. For example, if you are looking to demonstrate to your target audience how to buy a product from your website, a screenshot of your website accompanied by explanatory notes and arrows will enable the target audience to better understand how to use your website to access a certain product. You can also distribute your presentation to relevant social networking sites, including YouTube.

2. Alexa Rank

The Alexa Rank extension allows you to view the page rankings of all the sites that you visit. By adding this extension to your browsers, you will have access to vital information for your business. This information includes your own website's page ranking, the traffic to your website and to your competitors website(s), the Compete Rankings, indexed pages, backlink counts, social counts and information about the webmasters of the sites you visit. This information is particularly important in helping you to understand how your website ranks against competitors, and serves as a decision-making tool to help improve your website's rankings and traffic trends.

3. SendTab

SendTab is an extension that makes it easy to share links with people in your SendTab network. It is an effective tool for marketing and collaborating across the Internet, allowing you to send multiple links to your target audience/niche market, to both computers and cell phones.

4. Publish Sync

Publish Sync provides you with the tools to distribute your publications and content to your target audience through social networking sites. Through Publish Sync you can share your articles and links on Facebook, Twitter and Google+. When you add this extension to your Google Chrome browser, you can distribute your publications to all of your different contacts in the various social networking sites in one go. Through well-written expert content, this tool informs your target audience about you, your expertise and the value your business has to offer.

5. Y-slow

Having an effective website that allows visitors easy access is essential for your business. Y-slow is a Chrome extension that allows you to operate an efficient website by analyzing your website's speed and page rankings. Y-slow also shows you how your website ranks against your competitors in terms of efficiency, page ranking and quality backlinks. The extension offers analytical suggestions on the various ways that you can improve the overall speed, functionality and ranking of the website.

6. My Chrome Theme

My Chrome Theme allows you to customize themes and designs for your browsers and for your personal Google homepage. You can also send your custom themes to Google's theme directory and have them ranked. Homepages with the highest rank in Google's theme directory may also rank high in the search engines (particularly Google). With My Chrome Theme you can also create a distinctive URL for your customized themes and share it with others through Google +.

7. Color Zilla

Color Zilla is an extension that assists you in managing the visual aspects of your website – aspects that are essential in maintaining a professional looking site. This tool lets you test colors from any browser before applying them to a site. With its wide array of colors and hues, the tool allows you to choose any color pixel that you want on your page. Color Zilla is also useful in analyzing the intricate color detail of your website.

8. Bit.ly

Bit.ly is a URL shortener accessible from Google Chrome. This tool is effective in sending the shorter versions of links to social networking sites such as Twitter and Facebook. Thus, instead of sending out long links that may take up too much space or seem too long, Bit.ly allows you to send a compact link that will not put off the targeted receivers. This tool also allows you to track how many people are clicking on the link and sharing these links. When you sign up for a Bit.ly account, you can easily access the tracking statistics. Even without a Bit.ly account, you can still track the traffic trends by adding a plus (+) sign at the end of the URL whose traffic you are tracking.

9. Tweet Deck

Understanding how to use social networking sites for Internet marketing is important, especially for online businesses. When the number of people you are following on Twitter becomes too large, **Tweet Deck**'s grouping tool allows you to classify these people into distinctive groups for easier retrieval. **TwitScoop** brings you up to date with the trending news that is of interest to your business. Through the **12Seconds** feature, Tweet Deck allows you to use your web camera to create video clips lasting 12 seconds that you can send to your followers on Twitter. This is an effective way of staying connected and engaged with your target audience.

10. SEO Site Tools

SEO Site Tools is an indispensable tool that not only lets you view page rankings, but also displays information such as the number of daily new visitors to a site, backlinks, Page and Domain Authority and the popularity of a website in different countries.

Chapter 4
GATHERING INTERNET INTELLIGENCE

Gathering Internet intelligence is probably the main ingredient for a successful online experience. When I talk about "Internet intelligence," I refer to the right keywords to represent your business, information on your direct and indirect competitors, and industry trends. All of these can be searched using several of the Google Tools. Below I've listed the most important ones, and also provided some tips regarding their use.

SEARCH YOUR KEYWORDS

Everything starts with a search, and most people tend not to type in URLs anymore. It's all about "Googling" to find information, to buy a product or to look at the latest stock market trends.

Google Keyword Planner

Google Keyword Planner has now replaced Google Keyword Tool. In order to access it you need a Google AdWords account. There is no match type data for search volume, no device targeting, no global vs. local monthly searches anymore and no option to filter by closely related search terms. However the new Keyword Planner allows users to get keyword search volume data at city level with better geographic segmentation and the ability to bundle geographic regions. You can also upload up to 10,000 keywords from your own list to get performance data.

For more keywords ideas, go to Google Search, click on the icon representing a globe ("hide personal results") and start typing. As you can see, for each letter typed, **Google provides you with suggestions**. I would recommend that you write down those keywords that are relevant to your business and that are not yet on your list that we built earlier with the Google keyword tool.

Still in Google Search, scroll down to the bottom of the search results and check if there are any related terms you can add to your list. "**Related Searches**" can also be accessed from the left-hand side by clicking on "More search tools."

SEARCH YOUR COMPETITION

You've built your keyword list – now let's look now at how easy or hard is to rank (the position of your site in Google

Search) for these keywords. Still in Google Search, type your keyword within quotation marks (i.e., "*Washington Plumbing Services*") to see how many sites are out there trying to rank for the same keyword. If there are more than 150,000 results, I would suggest focusing on other keywords, as the competition is too high and there is little chance of you showing up on the first page of Google. If there are under 150,000 results, then look at the first 5–10 sites listed and write down for each one your first impression when clicking through the site. Is there anything you'd like to improve upon? Or, is there anything you can learn from this competitor?

If you install one of the Chrome add-ons mentioned earlier in this book, you'll also be able to see more details about your competitor's site, such as Google page rank, Alexa rank, page and domain authority, backlinks and social popularity. You get this information directly from the toolbar.

Google AdPlanner

To spy on your competitors' data, Google has a great tool called **AdPlanner** that is now integrated with Google Display Network and that provides competitive information such as data metrics, demographics, related terms, audience interests and other sites visited. This is a free service for any domain/website you enter.

Google Finance

Google Finance allows you to go past the numbers and statistics of a company. You can access information about a company's management team, read the biographies of the company leaders and find out about their trade activities and their business model. By gaining insights about another business, you are better placed to identify the latent business-to-business opportunities.

SEARCH FOR INDUSTRY TRENDS

Google Trends

Google Trends compares different terms and provides trends based on criteria such as location and time. This is a wonderful tool showing you how well the keyword you use is doing. Plus, it shows you other keywords that are being used for the same keyword. You can see which country is searching for the keywords, images, news or products you'd like to target. You can search for results in the last 90 days, up to 10 years worth of retrospective information. For what was mostly researched every year, check out **Google Zeitgeist**.

Chapter 5
ESTABLISHING YOUR ONLINE PRESENCE

The website is the lifeline of your online business. How you design it will impact your brand name and, in the long term, your business bottom line. As you set up the website, you should consider several things: the website's goals, the type of message that you wish to relay to your target audience and the type of reaction you want your website to trigger in your target audience.

Google Sites vs. Blogger

Although Blogger and Sites are different platforms, businesses can use these services to reach out to existing customers and targeted audiences.

Blogger, the 7th most popular site in the world and Google's hosted blogging interface, provides users the ability to create blog posts and share them with the world. As a business tool, Blogger is an effective platform for interacting and connecting with your customers continuously and in real time.

Google Sites is one of Google's web-hosted applications that allows you to create a dynamic website that acts as an interface for collaboration between members of a team. Essentially, Google Sites allows small businesses to create a hosted website easily, and for free.

Below I've listed the differences and similarities between these two platforms and the ways in which you can use them to benefit your business.

Collaboration - As a component of the Google Apps suite, Google Sites allows users to collaborate on the creation and development of a website. Through the Sites interface, team members can share documents, make presentations and have conversations in real time. Users who have access to the site can post comments and make edits to the various content that is available on the site. For a business, this type of collaboration makes employee interaction so much easier, even when everyone is in different locations. Additionally, the various sites and content saved on the interface are accessible anywhere, and from any computer, regardless of the availability of an Internet connection. The ability to collaborate with team members and sometimes customers is undeniably the main distinguishing feature between Blogger and Sites. Blogger is mostly a static platform that allows site administrators to post content on the interface. In contrast, Sites is a dynamic content management interface. Blogger is best suited purely for communication purposes through written content and embedded multimedia.

Access and Interaction - Although Google Sites serves as a dynamic web space for small businesses, it offers limited interactions with customers. With Sites, it is possible to share entire pages with the public, or with a selected group of people. You may also choose to keep the site private and only accessible to you. Once the site is published and is accessible by public users, Sites does not provide a way for site owners to continuously engage with their customers. In Sites, free commenting is not entirely possible unless users have access to the site. On the other hand, Blogger is a more interactive space that allows customers and other blog readers to not only interact with the site owner, but also amongst themselves. And since its integration with Google+, it has become even more interactive, as it allows social interaction.

Customization - Both Blogger and Sites are easy to create and use, and because they are hosted programs, users do not require additional software or hardware to operate these interfaces. They both operate on a WYSIWYG (what you see is what you get) basis, making it easy for anyone without prior programming knowledge to use either of these tools. It is equally simple to deeply customize the templates of both Blogger and Sites to allow you to use these collaborative and interactive platforms in a way that meets your needs.

Internet Cloud - As a web-hosted application, Google Sites is accessible through cloud networking. This makes it possible to collaborate using this application regardless of one's location. Site's cloud networking also makes it possible to access the interface without an Internet connection. Cloud networking is equally applicable to Blogger, allowing a site administrator to publish posts even when you are offline. The "Mail-to-Blogger" feature makes it possible to use an email account to post and publish while you are on the go. Publishers can use their mobile phones to make blog postings on the Blogger interface. The Internet cloud network enables *Collaborators on Sites* and *Publishers on Blogger* to access their respective interfaces regardless of location and connectivity.

Domain Names - Professional domain names are important for businesses, as they offer credibility. Although Sites and Blogger are both hosted web-services, it is possible to use a customized company domain. Therefore, instead of your site or blog URL appearing as "company name.blogspot.com" or "companyname.sites.com," it will appear as "companyname.com."

Really Simple Syndication (RSS) Feed - RSS feeds are an essential tool for businesses that are looking for online visibility. RSS feeds make it possible for a business to reach target audiences much faster and on a regular basis. Blogger has an easy to install RSS feed that enables publishers to communicate with their customers, and to attract traffic back to their original link. In contrast, Google Sites does not have an RSS feed gadget. However, it is possible to use third party platforms to generate RSS feeds to and from the site. Businesses that are looking to integrate their RSS feeds into their Google Sites would have to make use of RSS feeds such as Feedity.com, Feedyes.com, Page2rss.com or Feed43.com.

Storage - Noticeably, Google Blogger has limited storage space compared to Google Sites' storage capacity. Blogger files are restricted to just 1MB per file (compared to Sites' file storage capacity of 10MB), and a site quota of 100MB per site. The Blogger image storage capacity is 300MB. The large Google Sites storage capacity makes it possible for collaborators to store more files and documents, which are accessible on the go. It is worth noting that the space quotas in Google Sites are adjustable according to the user's needs at an additional cost. However, it is also worth noting that, as with any free online storage space, free storage capacity is regularly reviewed, and will no doubt be increased in the future to meet with the ever-expanding storage needs of individuals and businesses and rapidly increasing file sizes.

Sitemaps

Sitemaps on a website help your visitors find the information they are looking for more easily, and tell search engines which pages they should index. You can **create a Sitemap** based on the Sitemap protocol or you can submit a text file or RSS/Atom feed as a Sitemap. For more information on creating a Sitemap – which can at first be quite a technical and scary process – search Google for "Sitemap." There are several step-by-step guides that simplify this for you. Once you get the hang of this, it is actually pretty straightforward.

Google Merchant Centre

Google Merchant Centre is a Google tool that allows online retailers to upload a product list to be used afterwards for **Google Commerce Search** and **Google Shopping,** and to attract more potential customers to your site.

Google Commerce Search is a tool that allows Internet users to have an interactive shopping experience similar to the one that Amazon or eBay offer. The following functionalities are available: instant search, real time inventory search, on-site complimentary product promotions and user engagement based product recommendations. The cost for such tool starts at $25,000 per year depending on your number of items and site traffic, so it is certainly not a cheap option, but can be incredibly effective for your business and worth considering for businesses that are already up and running, are profitable and want to take things to the next level.

Google Shopping

The previous Google Product Search has now a new name: "Google Shopping". Much more than just the name has changed, however. Google Shopping offers a new way to locate research and discover *where* to buy products locally and online. Other popular CSEs that people use include PriceGrabber, Amazon Product Ads, Nextag, Shopping.com, Become and Shopzilla. These CSEs list side by side, a myriad of specific offers from retailers online for savvy shoppers to compare based on customer reviews, shipping costs and item price.

Google Shopping launched in 2012 is providing a new business model in that only paying merchants will be listed in the product search results. This is a pretty big change for Google who previously viewed the idea of paying to obtain search results as a bad thing. Google has never decommissioned any of their search products that were previously free in favor of one that costs money.

The process has been somewhat simplified. Any merchant wishing to list their products with Google Shopping needs only to create a Product Listing Ad (PLA) within their Google AdWords account to participate. Creating Product Listing Ads requires an AdWords account (google.com/AdWords) along with a Merchant Center account (google.com/merchants). Product Listing Ads will appear in Google Search results as well as Google Shopping. Whenever a user submits a search query that pertains to an item included in the Merchant Center account, Google automatically displays the products that relate to it beside the associated image, product name and its price.

OPTIMIZATION TIPS

The most effective way to generate lots of free traffic to your web store is to optimize your Google Shopping data input. Here is how you can get started:

1. Add relevant information to your data feed - One of the most effective ways of boosting your visibility on the search result pages is to make your data feed rich with information. Some essential information to add includes:

> • **Cost of shipping** - Google Shopping lists allow customers to sort through merchants offering the best shipping deals. The cost of shipping is also shown in the search results. It is advisable to clearly indicate the shipping costs in your listings.

> • **Product Category** - Define the broad category that your product falls under. Also indicate the specific category or product type that your merchandise best fits. This information will allow Google to index your products faster and accurately.

2. Make use of Adwords labels - Integrate your product feed data with your Adwords campaign by adding Adwords labels to describe your products. For example, you can indicate your costlier products, allowing you to bid carefully for these products. You may also mark the products that do not cost much and then launch a competitive Adwords campaign for these products. When users search for your products, the cheaper products will appear in the search results, allowing you to have more visibility than your competitors.

3. Write compelling product descriptions - Instead of using generic descriptions, create your own unique and creative descriptions. Google prefers unique content as opposed to general and duplicated content; great content will enhance your SERPs visibility when compared to your competitors.

4. Optimize the product titles - In addition to creating compelling descriptions, the product titles should also be catchy and include relevant keywords describing your products. The title should have 70 characters at most.

5. Product images - Other than displaying great content for your products, it is equally important that any product images are clear and professional. Consumers want to see what they are shopping for and are less likely to purchase products they cannot see and thus cannot trust. Great product images will not only boost your visibility but will also enhance view to sale conversion rates.

6. Keep your data feed up to date - Rich data and updated data are favorites for Google. Updating your listings and data feed information shows that your store is actively managed. Updating also enables you to edit any information that may not be accurate, allowing your store to look professional and credible. Whenever you make any changes to your products for example, a change in prices or the (un) availability of the product, be sure that these changes are reflected in Google Shopping data feeds.

7. Makes use of product identifiers - Google uses product identifiers to list products and to place them in comparison charts. On the other hand, users utilize these comparison charts or lists to find the best deals for them. Using the unique identifiers allows your products to appear in the comparison charts. The important identifiers include the Universal Product Code, the product brand name and the manufacture part number.

8. Track the Google Shopping Traffic separately - Your online storefront will attract various sources of traffic, Google Shopping included. An effective method of improving your Google Shopping campaign is to track the incoming traffic separately from other traffic sources and inbound links. Google Analytics is a great tool that allows you to set parameters for the specific data you are looking to keep track of.

WHAT IS THE COST OF PRODUCT LISTING ADS?

Google uses a cost-per-click charge on all Product Listing Ads. For select US participants they will use a cost-per-acquisition percentage basis. Product listings do not use keywords so attributes from within your Merchant Center will define product targets. The products will be grouped by brand and product type.

WHAT MUST BE DONE TO GET STARTED?

To effectively establish and launch a Products Listing Ad campaign, four things are needed:

- **Step 1**: Set up and submit your data feed
- **Step 2:** Merge your Google AdWords with your Google Merchant Center accounts
- **Step 3:** Establish your Product Listing Ad (PLA) campaign within AdWords
- **Step 4:** Use Google Analytics to track your results

HOW TO SET UP AND SUBMIT YOUR DATA FEED

If you are already sending your data feed through the Google Merchant Center in the free Google Shopping program, there is good news: There won't be much to do to modify your data feed and conform it to the Product Listing Ads curriculum. You will have the standard Google Shopping Columns. You will need to add to them additional data feed fields to separate or differentiate your inventory for the Product Listing Ads setup.

Add the following four fields:

- **AdWords Grouping** - Arbitrarily grouping products to establish product filters to commit a campaign specifically to a group of products (product targets) to bid differently for that product group. This is needed if the merchant whishes to bid in a different way for a *group* of products or a subset of products in the CPA or CPC percentage application. The grouping holds only one value.

- **AdWords Labels -** These are used *only* for CPC ads, but are similar to AdWords Grouping. Multiple values can be applied here as well. You will need to separate them with commas.

- **AdWords Publish -** Indicate whether or not you choose particulars to be listed in the Ad Extension program and the Product Listing Ads.

- **AdWords Redirect -** Redirect traffic from Google Shopping Source to an additional URL. This field will most likely become obsolete as the program depreciates in the long term.

HOW TO SET UP YOUR PRODUCT LISTING AD CAMPAIGN IN ADWORDS

You can set up a Product Listing Ad campaign within a text ad campaign that already exists. Setting it up as a standalone campaign will provide the best chance for success within the platform. Here is how:

- Create a new campaign by logging onto AdWords
- Name it "Campaign Product Listing Ads" and establish the Geo Locations Target; enable Product Extensions and set your Bids/Budget
- To house your Product Listing Ads, create an Ad-group by selecting the "Product Listing Ad" option underneath the "create an ad" wizard (in the Ad-group menu)

- The only thing left to do to complete the process is to set your bids. Do these four things and you will have created your Product Listing Ads campaign, as well as your Ad-group and Ads

It is important to note two things here:

- **Promotion** - Product Listing Ads enable you to add promotional text within your ads, such as free shipping, for example. Here is your chance to promote the product, and where you can include any offer that may entice customers to purchase it.

- **Auto Targets** - These allow the focus to be on bidding around a particular group of products. The following five things will define them: type, brand, product conditions, AdWords Labels and AdWords Grouping.

Social Features - Google have released new additions to Google Shopping with the most significant changes being the social features. Now users can read reviews from their friends and social connections and also create and share their own product reviews. Google Shopping users can also easily see if those in their Google circles have reviewed a product that they are viewing. When the search results for a specific product appear, you can access the reviews under the

Reviews tab, which will display reviews from your social connections.

Google Wallet

Google Wallet is a Google hosted mobile application that allows users to store their credit cards and discount offers on their mobile phones and desktops. Both brick and mortar and online stores can use the Google Wallet feature to accept payments from their customers. For customers, this is an easy way to carry credit cards and coupon offers and to make payments. For businesses, allowing Google Wallet transactions is a great way of making your ecommerce site easy to use. The Google Wallet application is a "cloud" technology, meaning that a customer can use it anywhere as long as the merchant accepts this type of transaction. The application is powered by near field communication technology that makes it possible for users to just tap their mobile phones on Google Wallet and enable cashiers to allow for the transfer of funds.

To enable Google Wallet in your online store, you will need to sign up for a **Google Checkout Account** and introduce your domain name. You will also need to integrate your Checkout account with gadgets such as the "buy now tabs," "shopping carts" and other services such as Google Analytics.

As an online business, why should you integrate with Google Wallet?

Attract More Leads - When site users see that your site has a Google Wallet tab, they will recognize it as a secure place to make online payments.

Convert More Sales - The availability of a visible Google Wallet feature simplifies the process of online shopping for site users. This is especially applicable if site visitors have used Google Wallet before on your site; all a site user needs to do is to use his/her email address and password to finish their purchase. When a visitor enters their information once, they do not have to enter it again the next time they make a purchase. This offers site visitors and potential buyers a seamless and quick site experience.

Processing and Managing Orders - When you sign up for a Google Checkout account, you will receive notifications every time a customer places an online order. You have the option of processing orders through your own order processing and management mechanisms or through the

Google Checkout Merchant Center. After confirming the order details, and after the customer acknowledges a purchase, Google will authorize you to charge the buyer's credit card. It is recommended that online merchants using the Google Checkout application charge their orders within seven days of being authorized to charge the funds.

Tracking Customer Conversion - If you integrate your Google Checkout account with Google Analytics, you can have access to metrics on customer conversions. Another method of tracking your site's cart activities is by monitoring the ecommerce transactions on your site. Google Wallet allows you to configure your site shopping carts in such a way that transactions carried out through the shopping carts are recorded and made accessible through the ecommerce reports.

Funnels and Reports - Apart from tracking the ecommerce activities on your site, you may also monitor the number of visitors that are accessing your site and placing orders. Google Wallet allows you to create funnels and goals. As you set up your goals in Google Analytics, you must include the login page, the place order page and the order confirmation page. These pages will allow you to receive funnels reports on important aspects such as the number of buying visitors that are using Google Wallet, the conversion rate and the point that visitors abandon their carts before they complete a purchase. This can provide invaluable insights as to why customers are visiting your site, think about purchasing and then abandoning the transaction.

The next chapter will focus on how to optimize your web presence for Google.

Chapter 6
UNDERSTANDING THE POWER OF SEO

The Keys to Findability and Google's Algorithm

Owners of online businesses experience a very competitive market, and it can be difficult to get your online business presence noticed. That is why **SEM** *(search engine marketing)* – also called "paid search" – and **SEO** *(search engine optimization)* –also called "organic search" – have been a good resource for small businesses. With Google being the top worldwide search engine (source **Royal Pingdom**, March 2010), it is the most targeted place to be in the Internet marketing world.

Recently Royal Pingdom used data from **Alexa** and built a report where they listed the top 20 countries with the highest number of Internet users (these countries actually bring in 75% of worldwide traffic). Google came number #1 in 14 of these countries, while Facebook came number #1 in only 2 and is additionally number #1 in Malaysia and Singapore. Still in the same table, you can see that **Twitter** has a better position than Facebook in Japan, and possibly soon in Brazil.

As a note to the above report, Royal Pingdom didn't include all the Google services/sites, but only Google Search. Google has created a product for each query that one can make: Google Search (also called "Google Instant" or "Google Suggest"), YouTube for video search, Keyword Tool, Google Blog Search, Google Book Search, Google Product Search, Google Health Search, Google Images search, Google Maps, Google News, Google Finance and Google Accessible Search. The only Google product that has nothing to do with search is Google+, where people go to hang around and socially network. However, here you can also search for people sharing the same interests as you.

Google's mission statement is to *"organize the world's information and make it universally accessible and useful"* while respecting their *"don't be evil"* motto. For many people, that means needing to be able to get their website noticed through the various methods of search engine ranking that Google utilizes to organize the information that they have access to, so they can land on the first page for the keywords in their niche.

The ultimate goal for a website owner, however, no matter what kind of content they have, is not only to be on the first page of Google, but also to rank in the top three results of any search in their niche. Studies have shown that over 90% of people never progress past the top three to five search results on any given search (Source: Cornell University Eye-Tracking Analysis of SE Users' Behavior), and less than 4% go to the 2nd page.

Google updates their SEO algorithm about 500 times a year, and every few months there are major changes (http://www.seomoz.org/google-algorithm-change) that have had a big impact on a lot of sites. The most important ones are the Panda and the Penguin updates.

1. GOOGLE PANDA

According to Google, Panda is a penalty that targets an entire site for low quality content. The objective of this algorithm, that was implemented in February 2011, was to ensure that websites with poor quality would not appear at the top of Google search result pages. Being an algorithm that targets the entire page, it is not enough to have some good content on some pages and then continue to propagate poor content on the rest of the pages. The entire website is penalized for hosting low quality content. Panda also has the objective of keeping plagiarists from attaining higher rankings at the SERPs (search engine results pages) than the websites from which they copied the content. Google Panda undergoes various frequent updates to assess the new content that appears on websites. As a result of these updates, websites that escaped the previous updates will be assessed and penalized if poor quality is detected on their websites.

Tips to Avoid Google Panda Updates

Eliminate low quality or auto-generated web content from your site - Having low quality content on your website is a sure way of prompting the algorithms to lower your site rankings in search engines. To determine whether your content is low quality or not, consider if:

> • Your site displays duplicate content on the same topic, albeit with slightly varying keywords
>
> • The content is massed produced and is lacking in detail and attention
>
> • The articles are too brief without adding any real value
>
> • The content is full of factual and spelling errors

Create your own unique content - Even if you opt to undertake content curation, blend this with your own unique ideas that will offer value to your readers or target audience.

Offer your own opinions and provide inspiration to your audience.

Be an authority in your niche - One of the best ways to avoid being blacklisted by the Panda algorithm is proving that you are an expert in your field. When your content is authoritative, other websites that are equally authoritative will link to yours.

Use a single URL - Instead of using multiple URLs to direct site visitors to your home page, use just one to avoid being penalized based on content duplication. Make the URL less witty and friendlier to your target audience.

Moderate your ads - It is not useful to crowd your site with ads. This will not only deter users from staying in your site, they are also less likely to recommend it to other users. Of course, a site that is full of ads is also likely to rank low on authority and is more vulnerable to Panda penalties.

2. GOOGLE PENGUIN

Google introduced the Penguin updates on April 24 2012. A Penguin is an algorithm that targets spam content or webspam in an effort to lower the rankings of websites that use black hat SEO techniques to boost their own rankings at the search engines. Black hat SEO techniques such as keyword stuffing (over-optimization) or buying of back-links are unethical and they would certainly subject a site to Penguin penalties.

Tips for Protecting Your Site from Penguin Penalties

Avoid onsite keyword stuffing - While the use of keywords is important to increase your visibility at the search engines, overusing these keywords predisposes you to Penguin penalties. Instead of building content for the search engines, create content that humans can read naturally. It is advisable to keep your keyword density lower than 2-3%.

Avoid blatant abuse of backlinks - Google will penalize you if you try to trick the search engines by building backlinks to your website from one of your other sites. Google considers this an over optimization of your main site.

Check your link anchor text - Another over optimization culprit is the anchor text. Ensure that the anchor text links to relevant content- avoid hidden text techniques that mislead the readers and the search engine. Your site will be exposed to penguin penalties if there are too many links pointing towards a single anchor text.

Avoid too much onsite linking - While it is acceptable and valuable to link the pages in your site to each other, you might be subject to penalties if you overdo the internal linking. Be sure that none of the content on any page attracts too many onsite links.

Use appropriate heading systems for headings - Search engines are privy to H1 tags. Instead of stuffing your articles with more than one H1 tags, use h2 and h3 headings.

Avoid overuse of redirects - It might be tempting to use redirects to increase the revenues from ads or affiliate programs. Using redirects for the wrong reasons only makes your site vulnerable to Penguin penalties.

Avoid content duplication - Instead of stealing or copying content from other websites, create your own valuable and relevant content. However, be sure to generate new content frequently instead of reusing your existing content too much.

3. EXACT MATCH DOMAIN (EMD)

Exact Match Domains are essentially domain names that feature the exact keywords that a website is competing for at the search engine result pages. An example of an exact match domain would be socialmediabooks.com for a website that is looking to rank highly for the key phrase 'social media books.'

For a long while, this was one of the easiest and most convenient ways used by site owners to secure higher rankings and attract traffic to their sites. The use of exact match domains also meant that some website owners did not take the time to provide and update content that is relevant for site visitors. This resulted in many keyword domains that only had scrapped or low quality content ranking highly at the search engines. However, the introduction of the Exact Match Domain (EMD) updates by Google on September 26 2012 had the goal of de-ranking keyword domains that had low quality content and had previously appeared at the top of the search engines. Google considered these types of domains as spammy and undermining the usefulness of onsite optimization as well as valuable content. The Updates did not, however, sweep out all exact match domains and instead left out those keywords domains that offered content that is relevant to the keywords these websites are competing for.

Tips to Avoid EMD Penalties

The introduction of the EMD updates does not mean that webmasters should no longer use these types of domains. On the contrary, it is valuable and possible to have a keyword-optimized domain and to avoid being penalized.

Eliminate low quality content from your keyword domain website - What makes for low quality content? If you wrote content for the search engines instead of for your readers, then this low quality content will see you penalized by the upcoming EMD updates. The content on your website must be relevant to the keywords the website is competing for. It should also offer value to those who visit your website. Regularly update the website content.

Audit your inbound links - Unnatural links will also expose your EMD website to penalties. Check to see the source of all inbound links to your website to establish their trustworthiness. Eliminate all inbound links that undermine the trustworthiness of your website. At the same time, undertake an SEO optimization and ethical link building campaign. One great way to do this is to invest time in guest blogging.

Boost website trust - One effective way of boosting the trust factor for your website is to include social media buttons that allow readers to share your content. The more people share your content, the greater the trust your website will display. Note that people will not share poor content but will gladly share and recommend valuable content.

When it comes to EMD updates, trust seems to be the most important facet. As such, it is important to undertake measures that will ethically enhance the trust metric of your website. High quality, valuable content and social media presence are workable strategies to avoid penalization.

4. KNOWLEDGE GRAPH

Google introduced the Knowledge Graph in May 2012. The goal of this search tool is to assist web users to view summaries of their searches; these may include brief biographies as well as related family members, associates and other events that are related to the thing or person that a user is searching for. According to Google, the Knowledge Graph helps users to find the correct item, to access the most appropriate summary and to discover other related information about the primary query.

Through the Knowledge Graph, search is moving away from basic keyword searches and results to more specific and intelligent searches and results. This tool makes it possible for web users to find exactly what they are looking for and other related information that pertains to the query instead of sifting through many results that do not offer the exact information a user is searching for.

Since its introduction, the Knowledge Graph features a database of more than 500 million places, things and people. The Graph also indexes more than 4 billion attributes and related information that connect the people, place and things that one searches for.

What does this interconnection between search queries and search results mean for the website owner? Search optimization is increasingly becoming less about a focus on keywords and more about creating relevant content and developing a sense of correlation.

Knowledge Graph Best Practices for Securing Your Web Presence

Correlation - Web content is intricately interlinked. It is good practice that your own content refers to other pieces of content across the web to build that connectivity that is needed to enhance your own web presence. This is the essence of link building efforts that require you to refer to other authoritative sites in your content and for you to conversely build content that other authoritative sites will want to refer to in their own content. Ethical and strategic link building will go a long way in not only boosting your rankings but also making you more visible at the search engine result pages for related queries. In addition to launching a well thought out connectivity campaign, do not leave out social media because content sharing across these mediums also boosts your web presence.

Relevant content - Given that the data on the web is interlinked, making your content relevant and topical allows your content to be effectively interlinked with other pages and pieces of information across the web. As such, your content and website will be easily visible even when users search for related things, place or people.

Build Trust - Google is big on trust and the search engines are increasingly awarding trustworthy websites with better rankings and web visibility. The Knowledge Graph is about making search intelligent. However, it is also about availing trustworthy, authoritative and topical information when users query the search engines. Building trust for example through ethical ghost blogging for link building and encouraging social media sharing of your content can serve to make you more visible at the search engines.

5. PAGE RANK UPDATE

Google releases an update for the toolbar PageRank at least four times every year. PageRank is an index that measures several metrics to determine the level of reputation of a specific page. The PageRank is determined by the quality as well as the quantity of inbound links. In addition to the quality and quantity of links, other factors such as outbound links and the number of such links available in any given page, the positioning of these links will also have an impact on the page ranking. The real PageRank metrics do not appear on the PageRank toolbar. On the contrary, the toolbar translates the real PageRank metrics using a scale that ranges between 0 and 10. The main aim of PageRank updates from the point of view of Google is to lower the rankings of pages that primarily feature broken or unnatural inbound and outbound links.

What you Should Do to Avoid Being Penalized by Page Rank Updates

A good number of websites lose their PageRank because of using overt black-hat techniques such as link trading. The problem with selling outbound links or buying inbound links is that the links are not necessarily relevant to the site they are pointing to and the positioning may be out of place as well thereby undermining the visibility of the website. Webmasters involved in link selling have already seen a reduction in their PR.

Another reason why your blog or website is likely to have a lower PageRank is that its inbound links lack high PageRank or are simply low on quality. This means that the quality of sites pointing to your own site will impact on your PageRank. Here are a few things you can do to keep your PR from plummeting as a result ongoing updates.

Generation of valuable content - It is not enough to rewrite content that you pick up from other blogs and website. It is important that you show expertise in your niche or in the topics that you are writing about. Website owners are increasingly looking for blogs with great content to link to. The PageRank update is particularly keen on link quality and quantity. It is much better for your PR when few authoritative sites link to you than a host of low quality blogs and websites linking back to you.

Attend to your site links - Poor links that are no longer serving your site are a sure way for Google to penalize you and lower your PageRank. It is easy to overlook the health of your links for a long time only to be overwhelmed when your site pages are too many. A better approach is to frequently check if both the outbound and inbound links on your site are working. If they are not, remove them and find other suitable sites to link to. Make use of free plug-in tools and software such as brokenlinkcheck.com to assist you in looking for any poor links that could jeopardize your site's PR.

Page linking - Even as you attend to the inbound and outbound links, it is important to properly link each page to the other in your site. This calls for the correct usage of anchor texts to allow the search engine bots to assess and index your pages effectively.

Guest blogging and commenting - Tools such as CommentLuv allow you to comment on blogs that have high PR and to leave a link to your own site. It is important that you comment on sites that are relevant to your niche and that you offer valuable instead of spammy comments. Writing and publishing your post on other blogs as a guest blogger is also a great way to receive inbound links to your site. Blogs with a high PR will only accept high quality blog posts.

6. GOOGLE PAGE LAYOUT ALGORITHM

Google introduced the Page Layout Algorithm to target websites that place ads above the fold. The Page Layout Algorithm is also known as 'top heavy' or 'the above the fold' updates. On your website, above the fold is the upper most section that does not require a site visitor to scroll downwards so that they will not see the ads. The updates were introduced at the start of 2012 following complaints from searchers who lamented about sites that featured more ads than they did any valuable content.

As such, the algorithm penalizes websites that feature above the fold ads and awards those with proper content with well-balanced ratio of ads. Sites with ads above the fold will experience lower rankings following the Google updates.

What you Should Do to Avoid Being Penalized

While this update may not seem as severe as the Panda or Penguin updates, Google is keen to serve quality content websites to searchers as opposed to sites that are flooded with ads. This does not mean that websites cannot host ads anymore; the point is to balance the amount of ads and to focus on offering quality content.

Pay attention to design - Undoubtedly, gone are the days when you could design your site the way you wanted to. To avoid page layout algorithm penalties, it is best to place as few ads at the top as possible. If the first thing that your site visitors see is ads, they are less likely to see your site as a trustworthy source of information. If your site does not demonstrate trust, Google is likely to penalize you with lower rankings and diminished traffic.

Check your links - The web is admittedly interconnected and this could not be truer in these times of various Google updates. If your site links to sites that have been negatively impacted, it is likely that your site will be afflicted by lower rankings and reduced traffic. It is a good idea to re-evaluate your links to make sure that you are linking to and are linked to sites that comply with the page layout requirements for ads.

Amend your ads - Lastly, if your site displays ads above the fold, you need to eliminate these. Google does not say how they determine if a site has gone too far with the ads; they leave this to the site owner to decide. Make use of the Google Browser size tool to see how site visitors will view your site in terms of content vs. ads. If there are too many ads when they access your site, it is an indication to reduce these ads.

7. LINK DISAVOWAL TOOL

Google, like Bing, launched the link disavowal tool allowing webmasters to remove bad inbound links that may affect their site rankings. Even though your own website may have quality content and links outwards to authoritative sites, some spammers whose sites are of low quality may link to your site. This will certainly affect your site rankings at the search engine result pages.

The tool essentially works by uploading a file that features the URLs that are pointing to your site and that you want to disavow. Webmasters also have the option of disavowing all links that come from a certain domain altogether.

How to Effectively Use the Link Disavowal Tool

Take your time before disavowing links - This will call for greater research on your end. Wanting to remove a link off your site entails more than just looking at the domain name. You also want to consider other factors such as exact match domain issues and links that simply appear unnatural. Only use the tool if you have experienced a significant loss in site rankings (you have been penalized through other Google updates), you have received a warning from Google about the links pointing to your site or someone is out rightly using black-hat techniques against your site. The problem with rushing to eliminate every suspicious link before really researching the value (or lack of) the link is that you are likely to damage your site rankings altogether.

Use only when necessary - The link disavowal risk does not take away your job of finding bad links and actually removing them. It is best to only use the tools to eliminate those links that you have in fact tried to remove from your site. There is no guarantee that Google will in fact remove the links from your site and within the shortest time. It is also a fallacy to use the tool thinking that it will solve the entire site ranking problems; even though bad links can impact your site ranking, other factors could also have a negative impact on your rankings at the SERPs (search engine results pages).

Fill in the correct details - Filling in the wrong URLs or domains could have permanent damage on your site. For the disavowal tool to work, you need to be signed in as the Owner of your site from the Google Webmaster navigation bar. Once you are logged in, include a plain text file and a single domain in each line. If you start your line with a hashtag this means that the line is a comment. If you include the term "domain", the entire domain will be disavowed.

Adopt an effective link building strategy - Prior to using the disavowal tool, it is better to build as many good links as possible. This way, there will be more good links than bad links and you will spend less time fighting off the bad links. There are numerous ways to build inbound links including encouraging customers and industry leaders to comment or offer a review of your products and services.

8. THE ROLE OF SOCIAL BOOKMARKING IN SEO AFTER PANDA/PENGUIN/EMD AND ALL THE UPDATES

For a long time now, webmasters have used social bookmarking as one of the simplest sources of back-links to their sites and blogs. All one has to do is create and issue a title, submit a URL link, add a description and spruce it up with some tags and a backlink would be created to your site. However, with the onslaught on website brought about by the various Google updates, the primary concern is whether social bookmarking is still a significant, reliable and legitimate method to use in your link building and SEO strategy.

The truth is that website owners must be very careful about how they use social bookmarks as part of their link building and SEO plan. Undoubtedly you can generate clean do-follow links from social bookmarking. However, these links will not necessarily boost your page rankings dramatically just as they are. A better approach would be to use the popular or well-known social bookmarking sites to regularly post relevant content that will attract a following or a community of other users who will not only interact with your content but will also share across other social networks.

In the era of 'jarring and jolting' Google updates, quality content and quality links are the most important determinants of a site's rankings. As seen, links from social bookmarks do not have any value in themselves. It would be more beneficial if you determined your audience and then develop content that will interest them. The larger your community, the more trustworthy you set yourself to be and this will translate to better site rankings.

Social bookmarking has not lost its importance following the Google updates. In fact, it could be more important than ever because the SEO, content creation and link building landscape has changed dramatically; it is no longer about chasing links and doing anything to remain top at the SERPs. It is now more about connecting with users through content curation and creating valuable content that will appeal to your human audience. This is where social bookmarking sites such as StumbleUpon, Delicious and Digg and others come into play.

Social bookmarking platform will still have the potent effect of making the best content viral. Penguin, Panda, EMD and most other updates are geared toward encouraging webmasters to develop content that is readable, accessible and valuable to humans. Social bookmarking sites, in a way, award site or content owners who produce the best content. Social bookmarking users will normally rate the content posted on the platform. Great content receives great rankings and poor content is ranked poorly. These community ratings could significantly increase your website's popularity and consequently boost your site's rankings at the SERPs.

Today, the role or benefits of social bookmarking can be seen as threefold:

- Traffic generation
- Enabling fans, readers, customers and your social connections to share your
- Boosting your social visibility

It is a fact that social network activities will continue to impact on a site's rankings at the search result pages. The more people share your content, the more you, your site and business is perceived as credible enough to warrant better search rankings.

To keep up with the latest on Google Algorithm Changes, check out: moz.com/google-algorithm-change.

Knowing how Google ranks websites is so important as **with traffic you get visitors, with visitors you can get customers, and from customers you get revenue**.

- **Paid** - Done through AdWords, paid rankings are very fast, as you can get to the top of the sponsored searches within minutes. However, Google stops showing you once you've stopped paying for the clicks. In AdWords, relevancy and high bids are the essential factors for your ranking in the top positions. Ads at the top get more traffic than those at the right. The ideal positions for your ads are between 2nd and 6th place, as people tend to click before they read the entire ad, and the ads in the first position usually get a lot of unqualified traffic. As mentioned previously in this book, this can be a very expensive approach to marketing your site.

• **Organic** - This is free, and is the purest form of online marketing with Google, but it can take time and it needs to be done with the Google algorithm in mind. However, once it is done, it can last forever. That's why it can be even more valuable than the paid method and is my favored approach when marketing any website. You do, however, need to understand Google and know what you're doing for this to be effective. Following the steps in this book should be a great starting place.

Note: As this chapter is dedicated to organic rankings, paid rankings will be discussed later in this book.

To make your website show in Google organic searches, you need to consider the three primary keys to findability that Google utilizes when ranking websites. Master these and your site will always be at the top.

First, Focus on CONTENT (on-Page SEO)

Knowing that 16% of all the Google daily searches are new (source: **Google Internal Data**), one of your main areas of focus should be to provide useful content on your site for your users and have a site that is easily readable by the search engines. SEO writing is a tough cookie to crack, because you've got to use your preferred keywords in such a way that they do not appear as if you were writing to boost your rankings.

If you've got content that people will find interesting, they will return and link to it, and Google will award you with a better ranking. If you've got content that looks like it came out of an article spinner and therefore is less readable in the eyes of Google, you are attempting to spam your visitors and therefore Google will drop your ranking, as this violates their mission statement. Your keyword shouldn't repeat more than three times (at the beginning, in the middle and at the end) in a 500- to 1000-word article. Put your keyword in bold or italic and also use variations of it. It is also worth noting that websites that can be very pleasing on the eye, such as those created with Flash, are not always the most favored by Google. Sometimes keeping things simple is more effective for Google ranking.

Second, Focus on LINKS Coming into Your Website (off-Page SEO)

Google ranks sites by the votes (also called "backlinks") it gets from other sites. These "backlinks" are a critical component to the ranking feature because they are an indicator to the Google virtual crawlers that your website has some sort of relevance. They also make your website look like a hub of activity, which again makes your website appear to contain more valuable content. Links from "authority sites" such as sites with high PR, gov. or edu, are called "juice links." To find .edu and gov. sites to link from, type in Google: *"keyword phrase" inurl: blog site:.edu or "keyword phrase" inurl: blog site:.edu.gov*

And Third, Focus on SOCIALIZATION

"Socialization" is when your own readers, customers or users spread the word about you on social media. This is also called amplification, and scores you extra socialization points when it comes to search engine rankings. Have you ever liked a Facebook page and then had a box pop up that says something like *"Share you liked us on your Timeline?"* Facebook shares and likes, Tweets, Pinterest pins, repins and likes and Google+1s (votes) are now becoming important metrics for analyzing the popularity of a website.

The Google+ button (served 5 billion times a day – source: Google Internal Data) is a another feature in search just like the Facebook or Twitter buttons, and is meant to help people discover and share with their social circles content that they like or find relevant. Google has publicly stated that they give preference to websites with the +1 box clicked multiple times, as each click is considered to be similar to a vote for that page. Any user with a Gmail account can +1 when they are logged into their account, and all the +1s clicked will appear in their Google+ profile. As a site owner, you can't offer anything in exchange for a +1 (as commercial Facebook users have done in the past, with promises such as "'like' us to receive…"). This has to be natural.

There are three ways to engage with a +1 button:

> • **+1 from search results** that could indirectly affect website rankings. Like the reviews on an Amazon page that can influence someone's decision to buy or not buy a certain product, the +1s in Search can have an impact on click-throughs, and therefore on

Google rankings. The +1s can also have an influence on personalized results (when someone is logged into their Gmail account). People from the same circle, searching for the same topic, will be getting the +1s at the top of their results, and they are most likely to click on them knowing that they were endorsed by someone they know.

• **+1 from a web page button** that helps a web page get easier votes from visitors. I suggest you add the +1 button on each page of your website, and not just on the homepage. The total number of social votes (+1s included) of a page will appear beside your social buttons, as in the example below from Mashable that includes social buttons for Likes, Tweets, +1s, Linkedin Shares, Pin It and Stumble Upons.

• **+1 from a Google+ profile or business page** that helps with the popularity of that post in Google+.

All three keys to findability work hand in hand to give you the best website ranking in your niche for your preferred keywords. You can boost your ranking with just one or two out of the three, but to maximize your findability, you need to have all three working simultaneously. Without relevant content, you won't get repeat customers. Without backlinks, you won't get new traffic and get ranked as you could. Also, the social media buttons (called "word of mouth" in the digital world) let customers do the work for you and share your expertise. So when you are planning your next website, keep in mind Google's mission statement and these tips, and you'll be #1 in no time.

How Google Search Plus Your World Is Changing SEO

Before reading further, I invite you to watch a great video that explains well the use of Google Search Plus Your World (youtu.be/8Z9TTBxarbs). Google Search Plus Your World (Gs+Yw) is a free web-hosted platform launched in January 2012 that seeks to bring together the social platform that is Google+ with Google Search. This integration allows users to personalize their search results and to have access to universal results as well.

The main features that make up the Gs+Yw platform include:

> • **Personalized Results** - This feature allows you to have access to information that you have generated. As such, you can have access to photos and content

that you have posted, and those that others have shared with you. When you place a query in the search engines, you will be able to see these personalized results on your Gs+Yw page.

• **Profiles in Search** - This feature allows you to use Google Search to locate and find specific people. These might be people that you are close to, including family and friends. You may also locate past and present clients, and follow people in your industry that you might be interested in.

• **People and Pages** - This feature complements the "profiles in search feature." It lets you find people in a specific niche market. You can access their Google+ profiles and their complete pages. Once you locate these people in your stated area of interest, you can follow them on the social community platform.

As you can see, Google Search Plus Your World is a great platform that allows you to stay abreast of industry trends and connect with the most influential people in your niche market. This means that, as a business, you have access to trending topics in your field and expert opinion from trendsetters in your niche industry.

The Advantages of an International Approach

It is easy to assume that only large multi-national companies optimize their websites for the different countries they are based in and for their multi-lingual markets. However, even smaller businesses that are scaling their operations to go global can optimize based on country and language. Here are several factors to take into consideration when you launch your global and digital business.

1. Research

When you target foreign countries, it is very important that you localize your SEO. People seem to trust more a site that is written in their own language. Also look carefully at the local online search behaviours and how the culture interacts with the web. While Google is the main player in most countries around the world, you should not ignore *local search engines* and try to optimize for each one. Besides Google, Bing and Yahoo, the most important local search engines are: Baidu in China, Yandex in Russia, Naver in South Korea, Rediff in India and Seznam in Czech Republic.

To search in Google within a specific country and language, I suggest you tailor your URL so you only get results for that specific territory or language. So if, for example, you were to search in Spain (gl = geographic location) for Spanish results (hl = host language) regarding "Medios de Comunicación" (q = query), you'd have to type the following URL into the search bar:

https://www.google.com/search?gl=es&hl=es&q=Medios de Comunicación

Similar results to this can also be obtained by using the **Google Global Chrome Extension** that you need to install on your computer.

As for targeted keywords, you must be careful when translating them into multiple languages, as the direct or indirect translations may vary radically from the English keywords. This requires extensive research on your part (using the methods shown earlier in this book) so that you have a comprehensive list of possible keywords (exact and related) that searchers are most likely to use to query the local search engines. Also, do not forget to search your competition on these keywords and see how easy it is to beat them.

2. Domain and Hosting

Once you define your local SEO strategy, you can buy a domain and hosting for your site. If you plan to target specific countries, I suggest you buy a local domain, such as .co.uk, .de, or .cn. If your intention is to target worldwide speakers of the same language, I suggest you add an extension to your domain for each language targeted, as shown in the examples below:

http://www.yourdomain.com/fr/content.html
http://www.fr.yourdomain.com/content.html

If you have content specific to a location, I suggest you **set up a geographic target in Webmaster tool** that will allow you to link pages with a geographical location even if your top-level domain (TLD) is geographically neutral, such as .com or .net.

As for the hosting, I recommend you host your website locally (same country as your target market) for optimum upload speed and reliability.

3. Content/on-Page SEO

Here is a list of the most-spoken international languages, according to Nationsonline.org. These are a combination of first and second language speakers.

- Mandarin - approx. 1,052 million speakers
- English - approx. 508 million speakers
- Hindi - approx. 487 million speakers
- Spanish - approx. 417 million speakers
- Arabic - approx.280 million speakers
- Russian - approx. 277 million speakers
- Bengali - approx. 207 million speakers
- Portuguese – approx. 191 million speakers
- French – approx. 128 million speakers
- German - approx. 128 million speakers
- Japanese - approx. 126 million speakers

Whatever language you chose to have on your site, please try not to use automatic translations. An automatic translation could be used in your market research to better understand what your competitors in different countries do, but if you are looking for a high quality translation for your site I recommend using a professional translator.

Whichever search engine you decide to target, you need to remember that the basic SEO rules such as good quality content and links from sites with high ranks will still apply. To help you in your research, each major search engine has their own keyword tool so you can check traffic volume for your targeted keywords.

Below I provide some tips in case you decide to optimize for Baidu or Yandex. Just so you know, both search engines rank content written in the local language higher than foreign languages.

Yandex

Launched: 1997

Worldwide Alexa rank: #23

Market domination: Russia

Keyword research tool: wordstat.yandex.ru

Good to know:

- Yandex prefers local sites, which makes it easier for small local businesses to rank higher in their area
- Both inbound links with high TCI ("Thematic Citation Index," similar to Page Rank) and outbound links count. However, links from forums and directories that are not moderated are not taken into consideration.

- As with Google, fresh and original content is rewarded. Additionally, in Yandex, for a site to rank high the content has to have good grammar and quality authoring.

- Press releases are also considered and the best press release distribution services are InterFAx and InFox

Baidu

Launched: 2000

Worldwide Alexa rank: #5

Market domination: China

Keyword research tool: index.baidu.com

Good to know:

- The more links, the better. Link quantity is more important that link quality.

- Local domain name and hosting are required. In order for your site to operate in China, an **ICP certificate** is required. As data centers from Hong Kong rank well on Baidu, my suggestion would be to host your site in Hong Kong. In this way, you'll be exempt from getting the ICP license.

- Write regular good quality content in simplified Chinese and put it at the top of the page.

- Optimize your title, description and image alt tags based on your Chinese keywords.

- Avoid Flash and Javascript, as Google can't read it very well, and often not at all.

4. Local Link Building

If you want to rank high on a search engine your links must be relevant and come from local domains. It is not enough to create a webpage for your target country or language. Just as you would engage in a link building campaign for your country website, it is also important that you optimize the pages for other countries and languages through local link building. This will require you to build rapport with local industry leaders in your niche and customers to encourage them to review, mention, comment and point to your site and the products your business offers. This will allow you to build local credibility thereby boosting your site rankings and subsequently attracting more traffic to your international pages.

5. Advertising

In addition to optimizing your keywords, you should also consider optimizing your ads in such a way that they are geo-specific. Your target audience is more likely to click through an ad that literally speaks to them through their respective language. Brands such as Nike are known in virtually every country; this is because the sports gear and personal apparel that are the main products from Nike are tailored to have both a local and international appeal. Nike's campaigns are hardly ever the same from country to country. Instead, they tend to mesh well with the local trends, needs and tastes of the countries they serve. Global marketing campaigns entail reaching out to the local people in the countries that your business serves. It is essential to localize your product offering and your brand in such a way that the local people can relate to it. Global campaigns make brands that are known by just a handful of people become internationally recognized.

Chapter 7
INTERACTING WITH YOUR COMMUNITY

Starting an online business and establishing a positive presence requires adequate planning and research. The online marketplace is very competitive and every day there is a new business that is seeking to launch online. This is partly because there are very low entry barriers to the market, and just about anyone can launch their business online. However, becoming and staying successful requires more than just a website. You need a digital strategy that will ensure that you are attracting adequate and relevant traffic to your site to generate profits. Developing a winning digital strategy to launch your business will vary depending on your goals. However, here are a couple of Google tools that will help you get started in the online market place.

Google+

Google+ is a Google hosted social networking platform that was launched in June 2011 and already has 100 million users (Facebook – 900 million, Twitter – 500 million, Pinterest – 20 million).

The top markets for Google+ are: US, India, France, Brazil and Japan (**comScore**, March 2012).

More than one million Google+ Business Pages have been created since its launch in November 2011. Google+ allows businesses as well individuals to network and share relevant content with others across the Google network, and with other social networks.

What differentiates Google+ from the other popular social networks are features such as **Circles** (for better segmentation and targeting), **Sparks** (to keep updated on the topics that interests you), **Hangouts** (a video chat service for up to 10 people at the same time), **+1 button** (similar to the "like" button in Facebook that can be found across the web in search results, on a Google+ page or on a website) and **integration with other Google services** (such as Gmail, Blogger, AdWords, Maps, Voice, etc.). While Facebook is a platform to interact with people you already know, Google+ is a place to find and engage with new people that you "want to know," and with whom you share common interests.

Based on a sample of about 100,000 Google+ profiles, the demographics were 70% male and 30% female.

Below you can find a social media short vocabulary for the top 4 social networks so you can compare them.

FACEBOOK

- Connect with people you know
- Two-way connecting
- News feed
- Update and share
- Friends
- Posts, Likes and Comments
- Comments and @mentions
- 1-on-1 video chat
- Send a message to a friend

TWITTER

- Broadcast events & news in real time
- One-way following
- Timeline
- Tweet or retweet
- Followers and Following
- Tweets and retweets
- @mentions and #hashtags
- Direct message (DM) or leave a message with @

PINTEREST

- Share visual content
- One-way following
- Pinboard
- Pin or repin
- Followers and Following
- Likes, pins and repins
- Comments, @mentions and #hashtags
- As Pinterest is usually linked to someone's site or their Facebook or Twitter accounts, you can contact them through these media. Otherwise, comment on one of their pins and ask for their contact details

GOOGLE+

- Share the right things with just the right people
- One-way following
- Stream
- Post, share or reshare
- People in circles
- Gplusses and comments
- Comments, @mentions and #hashtags. If someone you mention doesn't have a Google+ account, you have to add @ followed by their email and they will be notified

- You can also start a hangout about a post (Hangouts – multi-person video chat)
- Send direct emails to a user that has listed his email address, or post a message to the stream and limit share to one person

As with Facebook, in Google+ you can create "**Profiles**" or "**Pages**." The differences are listed below so you can decide for yourself, which one is the most appropriate for your business – or you can have both.

To switch between your *Personal Profile* and *Business Page* simply click on your profile image at the top-right corner.

- *Pages* are for businesses (local businesses or places, products or brands, companies, institutions or organizations, and arts, entertainment or sports). *Profiles* are for people, and if you are a freelancer, I highly recommend this option.

- *Pages* can't add people to circles until the page is added first or mentioned.

- *Pages* can have multiple administrators (up to 51 people can operate a Page, but only the owner can delete that page or transfer ownership from one person to another).

- The default privacy setting for elements on your *Business Page* is public. On *Profiles*, your full name (which is associated with the Gmail name account and can be changed a maximum of three times in two years) is the only required information that will be displayed publicly. However, you can choose whether to show up on search or not with "Help others find my profile in search results" – or if you want people from the web to email you without displaying your email ID.

- *Pages* have the +1 button, while *Profiles* don't. When somebody circles your Page, the Page gets an automatic +1 by that person

- *Profiles* can +1 Business Pages and any content on the Web with a +1 button, while *Business Pages* can't. However, *Pages* (just like Profiles) can +1 posts on Google+.

- *Profiles* can mention people in comments, whereas *Pages* can only mention people who've already added or mentioned them.

- *Profiles* can play games, *Business Pages* can't.

- *Pages* don't have the option to share to Extended circles.

- *Pages* don't receive notifications via email, text or in the Google bar – yet.

- *Pages* can't hangout on a mobile device.

- *Local pages* have special fields like maps that help people find the business' physical location.

Although Google+ is a new entrant in the social networking arena, it can prove to be a useful tool for online businesses when used properly. Here are some tips on how to use the Google+ platform in your business.

Setting up a Strong Profile

To make the most of Google+ you need to create a complete and strong profile, just as you would in other social networking platforms. An incomplete and weak profile will demonstrate incompetence on your part, and is likely to turn off your target audience. When setting up your profile, it is essential that you include a photo (250 pixels x 250 pixels) to give a face to your business. Describe yourself and your company at length (you have 5,000 words at your disposal). After setting up your profile, make sure to add a call to action by simply asking your target audience to share your profile across the Google platform in other social networks. Also, bear in mind that your name (business name), your tagline (elevator pitch), your occupation and your employer (only for Profiles) are all elements of your SEO, and therefore you need to make sure that they are set to be seen by anyone on the web. In the introduction content all the links are "dofollow" (the links get credit in the ranking process). In my experience, I've seen that it is much easier to get a better ranking position for Profiles than for a Page, as it is usually your name that you try to rank for.

Google Local

Google+ Local is the new Google Places and is now integrated with Google+. Before setting up a Google Local Page I suggest running a search on Google to see if your business is not already listed there. You can also run a search on business telephone numbers. If it finds a match, then you already have a Google+ page that needs to be claimed. Otherwise you need to create one from scratch. Go to **google.com/+/business** and click on "Create a Google+ page". Next select "Local Business or Place" and enter all the details required. Once your Page is live and your Business Profile complete, verify your email and domain. **Reviews received as a business on Zagat or Google+ circles will appear on your profile.**

Recently Google added a new feature to its local search results display called "Google Local Carousel". This means that when someone runs a local search a horizontal carousel of local places will be displayed at the top of the search results page followed by a map.

Subdivide Your Audience - It is possible to segment your social circle into groups (by relationship or by interest), allowing you to determine which type of content you should share with which type of group. By dividing contacts into "circles," you are essentially in the business of content and audience management. This approach lets you target your circles in an even more specialized way. Content that may be relevant and helpful to one of your circles may not necessarily be helpful and relevant to other people in other circles. To optimize content relevancy for a specific audience, segmentation will serve as a helpful approach. You may also divide your contacts into personal and business circles. One person can appear in more than one circle, and it is very easy to remove someone from a circle. Users will never know in which circle you put them, and if necessary you have the option to block users.

Design Best Practices - Continuing the theme of setting up your profile, you have the opportunity to upload visual content (static or animated) to the Scrapbook photos section in the header.

To create your banner I recommend using one of the free resources below:

- gplusbanners.com (create a free banner - 940 pixels x 180 pixels)

- gpluspic.com (slice your picture in 5 pieces just like BMW did – 125 pixels x 125 pixels each)

- gpluslogo.com (make a Google+ profile picture and banner using only one photo)

Creative Kit (open Google+'s Creative Kit by selecting a photo from your photo albums and then choose "**Edit**").

Note: All of the images from Google+ will show up in Google Images as well. That's why it is important that for each picture you add a keyword reach description, including your site URL. In the header there is a maximum of five pictures you can show. However, you can add more (and they can be seen if you click on the banner) and change with Picasa the order in which they appear (Picasa account>View All>Scrapbook Photos>Organize>put in the top five the pictures you want to show on your Google+ header). In Google+ you are not restricted as you are with Facebook when it comes to adding promotional images.

Technical Best Practices - Google+ and Sparks are now integrated with the Google search engine. For Google to crawl your site and allow users to find you and share your content, it is important to keep your site as simple as possible. Features such as cookies, DHTML, Flash and JavaScripts are likely to block your site from appearing in text browsers. Using the **Google Badge on your site** is a great method to inform your site visitors that you are active on Google+ and they can connect with you.

The "+1" feature after each post is helpful in giving your site a boost with search engines. By inserting the +1 feature in your website or blog you will allow site users to share it, create backlinks to your blog or site, and mention it across the social network platforms. According to Google's methods of ranking pages, the more your site is shared, linked and mentioned, the higher the chances that your pages will be ranked highly. Higher page rankings will go a long way in enhancing you business' online visibility and ultimately profitability.

The Google+ Share button (similar to the Facebook's share button) was recently launched and allows users to easily share site content they come across but do not want to endorse with a +1. *"When your visitors come across something* *interesting on your site, sometimes you want to encourage a simple endorsement (like +1). Other times, however, you want to help visitors share with their friends, right away. Today's new Google+ Share button lets you do just that,"* Rick Borovoy, product manager for Google+, wrote in a **blog post**. If you want to have a personalized URL for your Google+ page, I suggest you copy the long ID from your browser and then go to http://gplus.to where you can replace it with your name or your business name.

Quality Best Practices - It is important that your Google+ pages are built for people and not for search engine rankings. When creating content for your site with the aim of having it shared within and outside your Google+ social circle, ask yourself whether this content will be valuable to your target audience. It is also important that you avoid keyword stuffing and spamming, as this will negatively affect your page rankings. Instead, create content that is relevant to your users and they will feel comfortable sharing it.

Once you build your social circle and have a significant following on Google+, what is the best way to keep the followers interested? One approach that you can take is to publish posts on a regular basis. Ensure that the posts that you publish are not only shareable but also relevant to your target audience. Consistency in publishing these posts is also very important. If you want to reach as wide an audience as possible, consider making your posts publicly available. Content posted on "Extended Circles" is shared not only with your followers but also with the followers of your followers. You may also use segmentation to send specific posts to specific people in your circle. You can publish your own content or share great content you found on the web (also called "curated content"). Some sources for curated content would be Pinterest, Ted.com, YouTube, Storify.com, Scoop.it, Tumblr, StumbleUpon, etc.

When you share someone else's post you have the option to either keep the picture that goes with the post or select a different one from the same site. You can also upload your own picture or a royalty-free one from sites such as Google Images (search for something>then select advanced search>usage rights>free to use or share), **Flick Creative Commons** or **Wikimedia Commons**.

Keep Updated

> • *Sparks* is a feature of Google+ that allows you to aggregate content that interests you from the web and enables you to discuss this content with your social circle. Look at Sparks as a personal dashboard

that allows you easy access to the topics that interest you. The articles that interest you can be shared by including the +1 button in the article. If you are part of a business-to-business partnership, this is a good opportunity to perform your end of the B2B mutual promotion and marketing. As long as it is relevant content, your social circle will appreciate it.

• *Trending on Google+* is a feature integrated with Google+ that shows the most commented and re-shared articles. I suggest you check them often and +1 and comment on those that are of interest to you. You can also write something on those topics.

• *Preview Notifications:* As a business looking for profitably and establishing your online presence, it is advisable to always stay abreast of changes that take place across the social network platforms. The preview notification feature in Google+ bar allows you to take immediate action from the notifications menu, like commenting on a post or adding someone to a circle.

Get More Followers - Google+ is a great networking tool offering an excellent opportunity for you to connect with people who are already familiar with trends in your industry, or who matter the most to your business.

To expand your list of followers, I suggest two ways:

INVITE people from your other social media networks or email contacts to Google+. To import your Facebook contacts into Google+ you need a Yahoo email account where you can first import them. Once this is done, you need to go to Google+ and then "Find Friends" from Yahoo. When you invite a group of people, bear in mind that you can't invite more than 150 at a time. However, individual emailing is unlimited.

FOLLOW and they may follow you back. Once you've added someone to your circle you should interact with them: +1 the posts you like, comment on their posts and share great content. The maximum number of people you can circle is 5,000.

a) Use the search box and look for people you know, or search by category to find people to follow.
b) Follow people from the Google's Users Suggested List when you sign up for a Google+ account.
c) Check compiled lists of people to follow (please see the most popular below) to see if you can find anyone with the same interests as you, and also add yourself to those directories for people to follow you.

- *Chris Porter's database of circles* - <u>bit.ly/chrisporter</u>
- *Gabriel Vasile's list of best Google+ Circles ever shared* - <u>bit.ly/gabrielvasile</u>
- *Recommended users* - <u>bit.ly/recommendedgoogleplus</u>
- *Find People on Plus* - <u>findpeopleonplus.com</u>
- *Group As* - <u>group.as</u>
- *Find people on Google+* - <u>gglpls.com</u>
- *Women of Google+* - <u>womenofgplus.com</u>

Share a Circle with Others - When you click on a circle on the Google+ Circles page you will see three options: edit, share and delete. To share your circle, click on "share." Providing value to others will help increase your base of followers. To find shared circles, you can either type **"**shared a circle with you" in the Google+ search box or consult the lists below. The first includes posts with individual shared circles and the second ones with brands.

- <u>bit.ly/sharedcirclesongoogleplus</u>

Manage Circles - Audience management is very important when you take your business to the social networking platforms. Thousands of people will access your content. Some may make constructive comments, while some comments and feedback may be incorrect or inappropriate.

It is essential that you monitor what other people are saying about your business and product offering across the social network. Respond promptly, especially to false information, and clarify any contradictory information. It is also important that you share messages and communicate in a way that reflects your brand in a positive light.

Google+ Direct Connect - Google+ Direct is a feature that allows users to go straight to your Plus pages, view your profile and connect with your business. All you need to do is to have a Google+ page and a site URL that is verified to activate the Google+ direct features for your Google+ page. When people search for your business through a search engine and add a "+" followed by your business name, they will be taken directly to your Plus page, where they can access current posts and view your profile, as well as what your business has to offer. Activating Google+ direct is one really effective way of gaining online visibility.

Using +1 Metrics (Webmaster Tool) - Utilizing +1 metrics allows you to gain insights into the effectiveness of your social media campaign. This information will help you in making decisions about the direction of your social campaign. Use the activity page to see how many times your Google+ pages or web pages have been shared or +1'd. The

"Audience" report is helpful, as it provides you with information about the number of new users to your site and your Plus pages, where they are located, their age and their gender. Additionally, the +1 Search Impact report allows you to view the ways in which the +1 feature is influencing your site's page rankings in the search engines. Using this report will also give you insights into the number of pages on your site that engaged site users the most, as well as the site click-through rates.

Using Google+ Ripples - A Google+ Ripple is an interactive diagram that lets you see how your content is spreading and getting distributed by site users and the contacts in your social circle. You can access the Ripple diagram from the dropdown menu located right of the post whose ripple effect you are monitoring. This diagram also lets you see the people who are sharing your content the most (Influencers) and the time period during which the content was shared. You can use this information to make a connection with the influencers if you have not yet done so. This data can be seen for both your posts and the posts of those that you followed, and who shared them with you.

Note: Google+ does not show "Trending on Google+" on the home screen when logged in as a Business Page. You'll have to click on the

"Explore" icon on the left navigation ribbon to see what the trends are.

Social Plug-In Analytics - Google Analytics has recently launched a new set of reports called "Social Reports" to better measure the return on investment for in-site interactions (e.g., +1 button clicks) and off-site interactions (e.g., comments, posts and shares that happened on Google+). In order for these reports to be useful, you are required to set up goals. The Google+ Social Plug-in offers you insights regarding the activities of the social networks buttons on your site (+1s, Likes, Tweets, etc.). By using these analytics, you will see which buttons are clicked on the most by site users and what type of content users are sharing across the social networks. This information will allow you to determine the social plug-in buttons that are more useful to your site and those that need to be removed. These insights also allow you to determine the type of content that is most engaging for users so that you can keep creating this type of content. There is no integration setup required for +1 buttons, but for the other social sharing buttons such as Twitter, Facebook and Pinterest, you'll need to **modify your tracking code**.

Social Statistics - Social Statistics is a website that provides stats on how many people added you to their circles, how you have grown over time and where you rank in the list of popular Google+ users. It also tracks **the top 100 users** (currently Britney Spears is at the top with 2,876,117 followers) and **the most popular posts** on Google+. If you pay a one-off fee of $190, you can feature for a week on their "Featured users" section at the bottom right of their homepage. Their site gets 50,000 views a day on average, so this is something that you may wish to consider for significant exposure.

Customizing Snippets - A +snippet is the text that is displayed in Google search engines when someone in your social circle shares and distributes your content across the Google+ platform. It is possible to **customize these snippets** so that they display the specific message that you want displayed. For example, if your website is focused on selling health products, it is a good idea to include the picture and the name of each product, its benefits and perhaps the price of that particular product. As you customize your snippets, you will have to mark up your site's HTML using the **Schema tool**. Marking up your site with Schema enables Google robots to comprehend your site content and create the most relevant snippets. You will require basic comprehension of HTML to customize your snippets.

Plus One on Display Ads - Social networking platforms work based primarily on sharing and recommendations. To give more credibility to your display's ads, consider adding a +1 button to these ads. This will allow people to recommend your AdWords and AdSense ads to their friends and colleagues. When people receive recommendations about certain products, they are more likely to click through the advertisements than if there were no recommendations. By placing the +1 button on your ads, you will allow these ads to be shared and re-shared across multiple social networking platforms. To link your ads to your Google+ Business Page you need to **use social extensions**. For your information, you will not be charged when a user +1's one of your ads or clicks a link in a +1 annotation.

Finding a way of connecting with all the people in your social circle will go a long a way in helping you to manage your circles. Connecting your +1's entails bringing together the users on your site, those on your Google + page and those who click on your site ads. By connecting the people who are in your social circles, you will allow them to see aspects such as recommendations, product reviews and comments from other like-minded individuals.

Creating a Poll

To create a poll on Google+ you need to:

- Post a question and disable comments.

- Add potential replies yourself as separate comments to your post.

- Let people +1 their chosen answer.

- Keep track of the +1s you get on each answer.

- Close the post when you get enough answers, with a comment on the results.

Besides creating a poll, you can also use the "Want to ask your friends about...Ask on Google+" feature that appears at the bottom of your results on Google Search. When you click on "Ask on Google+" link, it will automatically create a post for you with some text that you can add to or edit. Once your post is ready, you can share it with your chosen circle.

CHROME EXTENSIONS

Start G+

With Start G+ you can read and reply to all your Facebook and Twitter updates right on your Google+'s stream. You can also post to Facebook and Twitter whenever you have something new to share with your Google+ circles, so there is no need anymore to switch between three different social networks. And this is not all. With Start G+ you can also import all your Facebook photos to Google+ – just visit startgoogleplus.com after you have installed the extension and click on "import your photos from Facebook." One other feature that the Chrome extension has is the integration with Gmail that allows a preview of your last 10 emails just from the Google toolbar.

Notification Count

If you want to get notified when someone is mentioning you on Google+ without having a tab opened, then get this Chrome extension that checks every minute for new notifications and displays the number on your toolbar.

+Photo zoom

+Photo Zoom is a Chrome extension that allows for viewing larger pictures right from your stream without leaving the page. Once you have installed the extension, you only need to hover over the image to get a larger version of it without compromising on quality.

Backup Your Google+ Data - To backup your Google+ data (profile, stream, circles and photos), you need to go to **http://google.com/takeout** and create an archive. Once this is done, you can download your files.

Hosting a Hangout - Google+ allows you to host a hangout with your social community and targeted audience. A hangout offers you a great opportunity to get personal with your customers and influential people in your industry. By hosting a hangout, you will be inviting people in your social circle and those in other social networking platforms to hold discussions and exchange ideas on various topics that may be of relevance to your business. You may also use Google+ hangouts to communicate with your team, whose members may be in remote locations. In this regard, Google+ acts as an interactive, cheap and easy method of communication.

There are three types of hangouts (please see the following table from Google), and **to get started** you need to install the Google Voice and Video Plugin. **Hangouts on Air** are the ones I highly recommend if your audience is higher than nine people, as even if the rest can't join and interact, they can watch the hangout live as a YouTube live stream. Once the hangout has ended, a recording will be placed on your Google+ page and YouTube channel. To edit your videos, I highly recommend **YouTube's video editor**, and if your video is longer than two hours you may need to download it, then edit and re-upload. To see stats on your video views, check your YouTube account.

Here are some sources for you to improve your hangout experience:

Recorded Hangouts
- *Google Analytics for Social Media -* bit.ly/googleanalyticsforsocialmedia
- *Cooking School: Pizza -* bit.ly/cookingschool
- *To find hangouts to join or schedule your own hangout check out -* gphangouts.com

YouTube

YouTube is the most popular video site in the world, and undoubtedly one of the most effective and widely used social media tools by both small and large businesses. The domain youtube.com was bought in 2005 and the website developed by three former PayPal employees. Twenty months later, in November 2006, the company was sold to Google for $1.65 billion. Today, while still censored in China, Iran, Libya, Tunisia and Turkmenistan, YouTube is number three worldwide in the top sites, behind Google.com and Facebook and ahead Yahoo, Baidu and Wikipedia. It is said that 11% of the global online consumer base is watching videos on their mobile devices (source: **YouTube Statistics**).

Let's take a look at some **stats** provided by YouTube itself:

- One hundred hours of video are uploaded every minute, or one hour of video is uploaded to YouTube every second.

- Over 1 billion users visit YouTube each month and watch over 6 billion hours.

- Roughly 70% of YouTube traffic comes from outside the US.

- There are thousands of full-length movies on YouTube.

- Around 10% of YouTube's videos are available in HD, which is more HD content than any other online video site.

- More than 50% of videos on YouTube have been rated or include comments from the community.

- One hundred million people take a social action on YouTube (likes, shares, comments, etc.) every week.

- Five Hundred years of YouTube video are watched every day on Facebook, and over 700 YouTube videos are shared on Twitter each minute.
- An auto-shared tweet results in six new youtube.com sessions on average, and there are more than 500 tweets per minute containing a YouTube link.

Pretty impressive, don't you think?

As we know, YouTube offers a free, dynamic platform that allows you to reach a wider audience in a cost effective manner. However, for this social marketing tool to work for you, you need to use it strategically. Here are some tips that will enable you to use YouTube to work for your business:

Keyword Usage - Keywords, also known as tags, are the main determinants of how well your video will rank in the organic search engines. Use your top keyword in your account username. Note that because YouTube is part of Google, the same page ranking criteria used for websites is also applicable for videos. So, use keywords that specifically describe what the video is about. YouTube allows you to use:

- 100 characters in the Title

- 120 characters in the Tags

- 5,000 characters in the Description

Choosing the right keywords to attach to your videos requires a lot of brainstorming, research and a strategic approach so that your content gains the appropriate publicity. Be sure to monitor the performance of the different videos you upload with regard to the tags you have assigned them.

For keywords/tags ideas, I recommend the following:

- Use the Google Keyword Planner, Google Search Suggestions or Google Related Searches

- Use the **YouTube Keyword Tool**

- Use the autocomplete suggestions from YouTube Search

Customizing Your Channel - Channel customization entails creating a YouTube campaign that appears professional and epitomizes your business brand and core services. A well customized channel will incorporate brand colors, information about your company and links to your website. Create your channel in a way that allows users to subscribe to the video so that they will always receive content from you. It is a good idea to ensure that your channel's interface is as simplified as possible for the users to know how to subscribe or how to go to your website. Subscriptions generated through a well-customized channel will allow you to interact further with your customers through email marketing campaigns and newsletters. When you set up your channel, pay attention in particular to the "About your channel" section. This is a very important feature, as it is here that you can describe your business and use your keywords. Beneath this section you can connect with other social networks such as Facebook, Twitter and Google+, and link to your site(s) (to make it clickable, you need to add "http" in front of your URL).

Creating Video Content - Every video on your channel is a new page, so the more videos, the more pages. While YouTube is an interactive tool that allows you to share content with the greater public, it is also a tool that you can use effectively for private purposes. If you choose to make your videos only viewable by a select number of people such as your employees, business associates or clients, only you and up to 50 other people will be able to view it. For example, you can create a YouTube video for people who have a subscribed membership to a program or service that you are offering. Instead of making such video content publicly available, you can make it exclusive only to your specific clients. This is a great way to use YouTube for training or presentation purposes.

Before starting to create your own videos, you need to decide what the purpose of the video is, the type of content you'll provide and how you'll create it. Here are some ideas to help you with this:

Purposes of a video:

- To build personal brand
- To make a direct sale
- To build your site readership
- To capture a lead
- To sell an affiliate product

Types of video content:

- Introduce your company and products
- Video testimonials
- Interviews with experts
- Instructional/how-to videos
- Recorded webinars
- Recordings of your Google+ hangouts
- Business updates
- Promotions

- Contests (two of the most popular contests on the Internet are "Dr. Pepper Cherry YouTube Dance Studio Contest" and "Project Virgle")
- Funny videos

Types of videos:

- **Talking Head** (you are the main character and in the background you can have a screenshot of your site)
- **Power Point Presentation + Audio** (For a microphone I would highly recommend **Blue Microphones**, which are very popular on Amazon)
- **Prezi** (a type of presentation that brings your video back to life by zooming in and out)
- **Screen Capture** (you can use **Camtasia**, **ScreenFlow** or iMovie for Mac)
- **GoAnimate** (create animated videos with characters without the need to draw them)
- **Paper Cuts** (e.g., **CommonCraft**)
- **Doodles** (e.g., **Sellamation**)
- For other tools to create and edit videos, I recommend checking **YouTube's Creator Hub**: youtube.com/yt/creators

Checking Trends - One last thing that you should also consider before starting to work on your video is to check trends. Creating content that responds to a demand is more likely to get you loads of views and go viral. To do this, you can check the following sources that YouTube has put at your disposal:

> • *YouTube Trends* (youtube-trends.blogspot.com) shows the latest trending videos and topics right now on YouTube. At the top there are four videos that generate more buzz, and these are updated everyday, twice a day, at 4am and 4pm Eastern Time.
>
> • *YouTube Trends Dashboard* (youtube.com/trendsdashboard) shows the "most viewed" and the "most shared" videos, by location and age. You can also compare several different metrics at the same time.
>
> • *YouTube Charts* (youtube.com/charts) shows the "most viewed," "most discussed," "most liked" and "top favorite" today, this week, this month and all time videos. My advice would be to subscribe to the popular ones in your category so you can keep up to date.

Optimizing Your Videos - It is not enough to simply use expensive equipment to produce a video. It is equally beneficial to optimize the video in a way that will attract your target audience.

- *Titles*: Develop creative titles for your videos using words that your target audience is likely to type in the search engines. Put your main keyword at the beginning of your title.

- *Description*: Other than the title, viewers will look at the description to see if the video will offer the information that they are looking for. Put your URL (with http:// so it makes it clickable) first in the description so people that want to click through to your site can see easily see it. Also, add a call to action.

- *Tags*: For each one of your keywords, check the top three to five videos and write down their tags. You can use some of them if you find them relevant to your video, but the first tag should always mirror your title. To get as many videos of yours as possible on the right side, I suggest you add some nonsense words or your company name as tags. In this way, if people chose to click on another video after seeing yours, they are more likely to click on another of your videos. Note that in your channel, only your videos will be visible. When watching a video outside a channel, suggestions for more videos to watch are shown in the column at the right. Still in the description, add a second URL with a link to your video in YouTube. You can only get that URL once your video is live. The purpose of this is that when someone embeds the video on their site, your video will still keep the description and you'll be getting a backlink to your video in YouTube. The more people that embed your video, the better you rank.

• *Thumbnails:* Use them wisely, as they serve as a navigational tool for your viewers. The images you use in your thumbnails should be attractive and directly related to your business's product offering. You can either upload a relevant image (available only for YouTube partners) or choose one of the three auto-generated thumbnails.

AudioSwap - In the background of your video you are not allowed to have any audio file for which you do not own the rights. YouTube uses Acoustic Finger Printing Software, similar to Shazam, to match any copywriting material. If copyrighted material is found, YouTube suggests some free music you can use. You can browse for audio files that have the same duration as your video. Once the song is selected, you can preview the whole video. It works well for slideshows.

Audio Captioning - Audio captioning is a strategy that allows you to reach as wide an audience as possible, and to meet the needs of your targeted audience. This process entails incorporating scripts into your videos, thus allowing those who cannot hear to still get the gist of your business. There are two ways that you can develop a transcript: You can use the **CaptionTube application** provided by Google, or you can create a transcript of your own and then use YouTube's speech recognition techniques to load the transcript of your video. Regardless of the approach you take to audio captioning, make sure that the transcription is well edited so that your business is able to maintain professionalism. The same technique can also be used to provide subtitles for your video.

Applying Annotations - Video Annotations is a tool that allows you to include interactive comments and information into your videos. Annotations act as snippets or creative stories that help your viewers to better understand the video. You have control over the annotations; you can add and remove them at anytime. One mistake that you should avoid making is the overuse of annotations, because this will only sidetrack users who will miss the important details in the video. This will lower the credibility of your content, and subsequently of your business. In these annotations you can add your keywords and a link to your site. To be able to link to your site, you'll need to use an app called **LinkedTube**.

Content Presentation and Organization - Organizing your content in a way that is accessible to viewers is essential. Instead of offering a continuous stream of video content, arrange your video uploads into categories that are easily understandable by the viewers. Remember that the main goal is to make the YouTube's interface as simple as possible for your online audiences. One way to organize your content is by using playlists. When creating playlists, assign unique keywords to these playlists so that they are relevant to the target audience. For example, you may separate your video content into categories such as how-to's, commercials and interviews. Creating keyword specific playlists will make it easier for viewers to navigate your video interface.

Optimizing Your Landing Page - A flawless transition from the YouTube video to your website is likely to improve conversion rates for the products and services that you are offering. It is not enough just to create an impressive video –

it is important that an equally impressive landing page follows up the quality of your video. When you mention your website's URL link in a video, the intention is to bring viewers to your site for further information on your product offerings. For this reason, your landing page needs to have a similar look and feel to the YouTube video. Optimize the landing page in such a way that it offers adequate information to meet the user's needs. When both your site and the video campaign impress users, it is likely that this will result in a higher conversion rate. This consistent visual approach should also be considered with any social networking strategy that you implement on Google+, Facebook, Twitter, etc.

Getting Views - Immediately after your video is uploaded to YouTube, you should let people in other social networks know about it. Once the video is on your Facebook wall, you can be the first one to "like" it and comment, encouraging other people to comment as well. To get all the videos registered in YouTube you should click on "share" and then choose the network or copy the URL to be shared and post it wherever you want. Your own views will also be counted, but this only works up to about 300 views. After that YouTube doesn't register them anymore.

To get the code to embed the video on your page, click on "embed." On a WordPress blog you need to copy the code from YouTube, create a new post and paste it into the html tab. Don't forget to uncheck the option "show suggested videos when the video finishes." Select "HTTPS" if you have a secure site. Leave un-checked the "privacy-enhanced mode" and the "old code" settings, and then choose how big you want the video to appear on your site.

Another way to increase your "views" is to look for popular videos in your industry. Watch them and then add a video comment. Note that with each one of your comments, you get a link to your channel.

Others options to increase your views would be to write a press release about your video and to distribute your video to other sites by using powerful tools such as **Traffic Geyser**, **TubeMogul** or **HeySpread**.

To insert a YouTube video into a PowerPoint presentation, I suggest first to convert the video to a WMV format. To extract audio from YouTube video, use an online tool called **Video2MP3**.

Comments and Ratings - The first comment on your videos should always come from you, starting a conversation and encouraging other people to comment. Find other people's related videos and comment. Hopefully they will return the favor. Note than no clickable link in the comments is allowed. If you can, post video comments, as they will be shown at the top of the text comments. For people to comment on your videos, you should have the option to "allow all comment with approval only" or "allow comments automatically" active. The same rule applies for video comments.

In addition to comments, you can also get "votes" (thumbs up, thumbs down). There are two types: for your video or for the comments received. The comments that get more votes will rank higher.

Encourage Viewer-Generated Content - Sometimes it is not entirely possible to generate video content all on your own. A good approach to take is to encourage your viewers to generate their own content and to upload it to your channel. Of course, the user-generated content should be related to what your business is about. Encouraging users to generate content for your channel is also an effective way of creating greater credibility for your campaign. It is not just you promoting a product, but other real people who are equally engaged in the campaign too.

Curated Videos - You can use curated videos as a way of creating visibility for your business without posting your own videos. This process entails gathering videos from other websites and from YouTube, creating a playlist for these videos and then distributing them to your targeted audience. This approach is particularly relevant if you have already networked with other players in the industry and have a working collaboration with them. From a business point of view, video curation is primarily a means of providing your viewers with valuable content. The type of information that you gather and distribute to your customers should be relevant to your own business.

YouTube Analytics (Formerly YouTube Insight) - YouTube Analytics is a valuable tool that helps you determine the success of your video campaigns and provides you with information such as the demographics of the people viewing your videos, which videos drive more views and subscriptions, how far people are watching a video, keywords typed by people on YouTube or Google search before getting to your video, on which sites your videos were embedded, how people got to your videos, etc. When you look at the traffic sources for a specific video, you can see that these links are clickable and bring you to the page of the video that had yours on the right-hand side as a suggested video. You could go and check their tags and comment on the video. Making use of this tool also allows you to monitor the time and days when your video receives the highest viewership.

In addition to the YouTube Analytics data on your videos, there is also the option of checking stats for your competitors' videos. You can see on which sites the video was embedded, how many views it has, if there were any views on mobile devices, if Google or YouTube searches brought any traffic to your video, etc. Once you've found out where your competitor's video was embedded, you can go and ask if you can get your video or article embedded there as well.

As Seen On is a feature that was implemented by YouTube in 2011. In this section you'll find listed one of the sites that embedded your video and has a lot of traffic. This is like a "give back" from YouTube to those that send a lot of traffic to video sites. If you come across this feature on any of the videos you are watching, try to contact the site owner and see if you can also embed your video.

YouTube Partnership Programs

1. Display advertisements with your videos: is much like the AdSense program that allows you to monetize your content. Prior to April 2012, people had to apply to be accepted. Now you only have to opt-in your channel for monetization. To be paid you need to associate your AdSense account. Your content has to be original and have at least one video enrolled in the program. So far, people from 20 countries can participate in the program: Argentina, Australia, Brazil, Canada, Colombia, Czech Republic, France, Germany, Ireland, Israel, Japan, Mexico, Netherlands, New Zealand, Poland, South Africa, Spain, Sweden, United Kingdom and the United States.

2. Offer videos for rent: You decide the price ($0.99 to $19.99) and the duration of rental (one day to unlimited duration). Have an AdSense Account linked to your YouTube account to get paid. People can't return the video and asked for a refund if they watched it entirely. Rentals are only available for US users and US partners. For people to pay for a rental, they need a Google Wallet account. You can create a trailer to promote your rentals.

3. Live-Streaming: that allows broadcasting in real time directly from an YouTube channel.

Other Great YouTube Resources to Check

- *TestTube* - <u>youtube.com/testtube</u> lists what's being tested at the moment in beta

- *PixelPipe* - <u>pixelpipe.com</u> is an online platform that allows you to publish photos, video, audio and text across dozens of online services.

- *QuietTube* - <u>quietube.com</u> removes everything surrounding a video (comments, annotations, advertising, etc.) and lets you watch the video in peace. You just need to drag a button to your toolbar (much like the "Pinterest" button) and you're sorted.

- *TubeChop* - <u>tubechop.com</u> allows you to crop a part of the video that interests you and share it with your social networks.

Google News

Google News is a web-based platform that collects news from different sources on the web and makes them available to users who subscribe to this platform. Google crawls over 50,000 news sources including blogs and websites to generate news and information that is of interest to you and your business. Using Google News as a tool for business enables you to remain current in your industry, to understand and meet your customer's needs and, most importantly, to maximize your bottom line. Here are some tips to help you make the best of the Google News platform.

PRESS RELEASES

Creating and distributing press releases is an important part of informing your customers and the wider public about your business. Press releases also increase visibility for your business when they are widely accessible. For Google to accept your company's press releases into their database, there are some features that must be present in the press releases.

Using Multimedia - Google Images attracts a large amount of traffic through search engines. It is said that 5.7% of all searches are image searches. You can take advantage of this by optimizing your press releases with images that are relevant to the content. Images are not only visually appealing – they will also rank you higher as Google crawls and indexes the various press releases available on the web. To ensure that your image is well optimized, use a keyword to create a brief description of the image. Additionally, be sure to use a precise name for the image file.

Linking - Proper linking of your press release ensures that it is adequately optimized for the search engines to rank it appropriately. When linking your press release to your site and other authoritative sites, it is important that you link deeper into these sites. This means that your anchor texts and hyperlinks should lead to pages other than the first page on the linked site. This approach ensures that both the linked-to pages and the entire website will have equally good rankings. It is also advisable to place some links at the start of the press release to enable search engine robots to easily crawl and index your press release. Use the anchor text on your press release to briefly elaborate on the content of the page that you are linking to and its relevance to the overall press release.

Press Release Format - Google has a very specific format that you should be keen to follow for your press release to be picked up by search engine spiders. Your headline should be brief and to the point (under 20 words) to enable the search engines to index your press release for higher rankings. Be sure to optimize your title with appropriate keywords. Generally, the content of your press release should range between 125 to 700 words. Remember that higher rankings and superior content will increase your chances of being aggregated into the Google News platform.

REQUIREMENTS FOR GETTING INTO GOOGLE NEWS

Other than using Google News as your source of aggregated information, you can be part of the news sources. Getting into Google News is a brand visibility strategy to consider as your business grows. Before Google accepts to index your site and content for worldwide distribution, you must qualify on certain fronts.

Quality Content - To get into Google News, it is important that you generate high quality content that is relevant to your audience. Generally, you should be able to submit news that is current and not outright hard marketing. Think of getting into Google News as a platform to inform your customers about the issues that are interesting to them, and not just to you; this could be about progression or changes in your business or in the industry.

Credibility - Establish authority and credibility by providing information about yourself and any contact that users can use to reach you upon reading your content. Customers are usually looking for a real person with whom they can interact about a product offering, or simply to make inquiries. When your content does not have a human face to it, it does not mean anything to customers who may be interested in what your business has to offer.

Ease of Use - The site URL you provide Google must not redirect users to a different site, otherwise this would make it difficult for users to interact with your site. Redirected sites will also make it difficult for Google to crawl and index your site.

REALLY SIMPLE SYNDICATION FEEDS (RSS FEEDS)

RSS feeds are an integral feature of the Google News platform, offering you an efficient way to access information that is relevant to your business. RSS feeds, when incorporated into your website, can also serve as a tool for distributing your own content to your targeted customers.

Creating RSS Feeds - As a publisher, you have control over the information that appears in your feed. You can choose to have full feeds or partial ones, depending on the direction of your RSS strategy. As you create your feeds, you must always have your customers and target market in mind. Taking this approach will help you determine the type of content to generate and how this will meet your customer's needs. On the technical aspect of creating, although you could do it manually, you will save more time by using a web and desktop application for syndicating your RSS feeds. Once you create the feed, send it to your sever.

Submitting Your Feeds - One approach to reaching a wider audience with your RSS feeds is to submit them to the Google News platform. You need to create a personal page or account, through which you can submit your feeds. To include your feed, simply select the "Add Content" link and then type in your feed's URL and click add. Google will submit your feed content to users who use criteria that match with your feed content. Other than Google, you may diversify your RSS strategy by submitting your feed to other RSS feed directories.

Promoting Your Feeds - Customers subscribe to feeds because they are looking for specific information. As an RSS publisher, your RSS strategy is greatly influenced by the quality of the content available in your feeds. How your content ranks in the search determines how many people will be attracted to subscribe to your feeds. For Google News to pick up your content, it is important that you optimize this content and make it relevant to your target audience. Making your feeds adequately unique to stand out from the competitive crowd is the best way to promote yourself to your customers.

Additionally, always remember to enhance your online visibility by creating a link between your feed and your site, and vice versa.

Full Feeds vs. Partial Feeds - Whether or not you use full or partial feeds depends on what you are trying to accomplish with your RSS feeds as a publisher. You might want to submit partial feeds to encourage readers to visit your site for the full content. On the other hand, a full feed submitted to your readers does not guarantee that they will follow the URL to you website, to view and purchase your product. Do not assume that partial feeds will result in higher click-through rates to your site, unless readers are very keen on your content. By making your feed content engaging, whether it is partial or full, you will be in a better position to increase click-through rates to your site.

Sharing Feeds - You can share feeds with your social network in an effort to spread the word about your product offerings. You can also share information that is as relevant to your social network circle as it is to your business.

When you receive news that might add value to your social network – including clients and target market information – utilize the share options to provide them with this information. You can embed comments on the feed stating why you find the feed interesting or relevant, and encourage them to visit your site. Think of feed sharing as a way of engaging with your clients and target audience, while at the same time soft selling your product offering.

AdSense for Feeds - You can use your feeds to generate a stream of revenue by participating in the AdSense for Feeds platform. This program is similar to other pay-per-click advertisement programs. Although monetizing your feed is entirely a business decision, you must also take into consideration the impression this might create with your targeted audience. Certainly, feeds that have a high number of subscribers are more likely to boost your bottom line. To monetize your feeds, Google requires that you have over 100 consistent subscribers. Optimizing your content for higher rankings and relevancy is a good approach to take, increasing your feed subscription base.

As it is very hard to get into Google News directly, I suggest you go to news.google.com and introduce your keyword. Look at the news sources in your results and try to submit your press releases to them. If these sites approve your press release, there is a good chance that you will show up on the Google News first page.

The next chapter will be all about AdWords, Google's most profitable product.

Chapter 8
ADWORDS: GROWING YOUR BUSINESS WITH PAID ADVERTISING

There are many ways to increase your overall business with Google, and as we've seen, mastering these tools can provide huge benefits. We'll now look at one of the most popular ways of marketing your business online and increasing traffic to your site.

AdWords is Google's pay-per-click advertisement plan. This program allows businesses to advertise their products and services online by creating a short advertisement pitch that is displayed on Google search pages, alongside the company URL. Businesses use keyword-rich pitches to gain higher rankings in the search engines. They also engage in a bidding process for the keywords they use for their advertisements. Every time users click on your advertisement and land on your website, Google will charge your business a set amount for this click.

Using AdWords can help you improve your business's visibility. If you have a well-managed AdWords campaign, it is likely that you will begin to see the rewards in terms of an increase in sales, or at least more customer inquiries. Here are some advanced AdWords tips that will boost your company visibility, help you save on your advertisement costs and convert potential customers into actual ones.

1. Analyze Your Competition - The first thing you want to do before you even start your AdWords campaign is to analyze the competition and know where you are in your industry. There are many powerful tools such as **spyfu.com** or **ispionage.com** that will help you to get an idea of which keywords your competitors are and are not using. These can help you to gauge where you need to start with your campaign.

2. Set up Your First Campaign - When you set up your first campaign, I suggest the following steps:

- **Search for keywords that define your products or services**

- Bear in mind that when people search the web, they take many different approaches with many different desired outcomes. As such, your ads should be addressing these different types of consumers: **awareness** (consumer searches for

general terms and the conversion is very low),
interest (consumer knows the product and in order
for them to click on your ad you need to include the
benefits), **evaluation** (consumer is interested in
learning more about a product, so in order for them
to click on your ad you need to include
specifications and features), **shopping phase**
(consumer is comparing products so you need to
include your USP) and **commitment** (at this stage
the consumer has all the information they need and
has decided to purchase). You also have **logical
searchers** that use words such as "how" and "why"
and **emotional searchers** that use words such as
"best," "latest," etc.

• **Group your keywords by putting similar words
together**

• **Create two ads per group**

• When one of your ads gets at least 200 clicks or
10,000 impressions, the second one, which is the
weakest, needs to be replaced with a new ad. When
creating your ads, bear in mind that the **first line or
the title** is attention-grabbing, the **second line**

should include the benefits of your product or service and the **third line** should include features and a call to action. Ads that convert better are those showing the benefits: "more money," "more freedom," "better lifestyle," etc. Exact numbers, discounts and question marks are also recommended to be included.

• **Include your keyword in the display URL that is different from the destination URL**

• **Use the Adwords Editor to manage your ad campaigns once they are live**

• **Start with a low daily budget** – between $25 and $100 – until you begin to understand what works and what does not. You can set up bids at the keyword level, campaign level or ad group level.

• Use only **exact match** (someone searches for a specific phrase, with no other terms in the query) and **phrase match** (someone searches on your exact phrase or with additional words before or after) when you start, so as to avoid spending money on **broad match** (your ad may show if a search query contains your keyword terms in any order, and possibly along with other terms).

• If your keywords do not get any impressions, pause them. If your ads do not get a lot of clicks, replace them. If you get a lot of click-throughs to your site but not many conversions, you may want to review your landing page.

3. Increase Conversion Rates by Optimizing the Landing Page - Your goal is to optimize your site's landing page so that it contains the information that your typical customers will be looking for. The landing page of your site plays a significant role in either encouraging customers to buy your products and services or turning them away to your competitors. Although the look of the page is an essential factor, the details and information contained are even more important. Ensure that your landing page contains Terms and Conditions, Privacy Policy, a Contact Us page, relevant keywords and solutions to keep users on the page. Also, ensure that the link you provide on the ad leads directly to the informational page and not to other web pages.

4. Utilize Geo-Setting Options - Geo-setting is a technique that allows you to narrow down your targeted niche market.

This means that the people who will click on your ad would be those that your product or services are targeted at. You can set your ad in a way that attracts specific customers, customers in a particular state or international customers. Geo-setting is especially important for a small business that is targeting a very narrow niche market in a particular location. A geo-setting strategy helps in managing your advertisement budget, as the customers who click on your ads are more relevant to your business.

5. Manage Return on Investment - Make your ad, keywords and landing pages relevant. Always try to make a minimal bid. This way your ad is likely to receive more specific clicks than general ones. Google uses the Quality Score to rank ads. The quality score that your adverts receive is determined by their relevancy, the content on your landing page and the amount that you bid for any given keyword. Although it might seem like a logical strategy, bidding high to attain the top page ranks is not always good for your ROI. On the contrary, it is likely that everyone will click on the first ad on the page, but then again your business is not targeting everybody, but in fact a smaller niche. This means that you will be paying more per click even though very few of these clicks convert into leads or sales.

6. Focus on Long Tail Keywords - One way of developing long tail keywords that are relevant to your campaign is to run a search query report to look for keyword searches that demonstrate more than a single click. After your search, combine these words with your existing list of keywords to bring out a more specific keyword. Using long tail keywords for your ads is particularly helpful if your Internet marketing campaign seems to have reached a plateau. This means that you are not generating as many sales and your pay-per-click costs cannot be justified by the number of sales. Long Tail keywords are specific words that target users who are in the late buying cycle. These users have already done their research and are likely to look for the best service provider from whom they can purchase a service or product.

7. Use Negative Keywords - Use "AdWords Keyword Tool" and "Search Terms" to look for negative keywords in your ad category. This requires a significant investment of time and research. Using negative keywords is an advanced method of keeping away general clickers and attracting specific users who are most likely looking to buy or make an inquiry. This ensures that you are not paying for clicks that will not lead to significant conversions. For example, by including a location in your advertisement, you are deterring general clickers and attracting customers in that specific location to click on your adverts and find out about your product offering.

8. Synchronize with Google Analytics - Google Analytics is an application that allows you to track the number of users to your site, the type of users who visit the site and how long they stay on the site. Google Analytics also helps you to determine which of your advertisement campaigns are doing well and which ones need optimization. Significant metrics include the keyword value, the quality of engagement that users have with your site, your best performing keywords and how well you are performing across the industry. Use these metrics to make fundamental decisions about optimizing your keywords, page content and user-site engagement. By synchronizing your AdWords account with Google Analytics, you will receive in-depth analysis of metrics that are significant to your business.

9. Use the Search Funnel Report - Getting clear information about your users' search behavior will help you in determining the best way to capture and convert them. Using funnel visualization reports will help you understand site users' behavior, and consequently move your advertisement campaign toward a more targeted approach. A funnel visualization report will give you insights into questions such as:

- What keywords are searchers using?
- At what point do they lose interest in your page and click on the back button?
- What conversion path do those who buy from you take, and can you duplicate this with other potential buyers?
- What keywords did they use?
- Which ones did they not use?

You can access funnel visualization reports from the "Goals" tab in Google Analytics to track conversion and impression paths.

10. Filter Unproductive Traffic - Unproductive traffic is a sign that your ad campaign is not highly targeted. All businesses – even those seemingly targeting the mass market – have a niche market in mind. Your ad campaign should have a targeted group of customers that are more likely to click on your advert and to buy or inquire about your product offering. This is what it means to filter unproductive traffic. One way to do this is to indicate a price in your ads. Let this price be very close to the target keyword. It is likely that only users who are already high in the buying cycle will click your ad and thus bring about a conversion.

11. Run Ads on the AdWords Display Network - You can choose where your ad will appear when you decide to participate in the display network. Choose sites that are relevant to your business and your campaign. The display network includes all the web pages that are part of the AdSense program. The display network allows you to place your advertisements on sites other than Google pages. Participating in the AdWords display network may be costlier than just appearing on Google search pages, but the returns on your ad campaign could be higher. Naturally, the sites you choose to display your ads on are those that your targeted customers are most likely to visit. Contextual targeting is a better approach when compared to placements where your advert can appear in any webpage in the display network.

12. Include Rich Media Ads - The Display Ad Builder that is accessible through your AdWords account is a good place to start with your rich media ad creation. This tool helps you in achieving the appropriate mix of image and text. Displaying ads with images is a great way to attract target customers. Visual displays, compared to purely text ads, tend to attract the eyes of web users. Using images should not distract you from building an effective text-based campaign. The text is what tells users what the image is about. To test how well your rich media ads are doing, launch a new campaign and also take some of your high performance text ads and incorporate them with image ads. Choose to place your rich media ads at the beginning or at the end of YouTube clips, or at the top head of web pages in the display network, through contextual targeting.

13. Lower Your Ad Position - Consider lowering the position of your ad to optimize the click-through rate. As seen earlier, an ad strategy that primarily seeks to place your advertisements at the top of the page is not necessarily a foolproof strategy. The click-through rate is the rate at which (relevant) users are clicking on your ads with the aim of buying, subscribing or making inquiries. Lowering your ad position might seem like sabotaging business visibility, but in this way you will be protecting your bottom line. An effective technique is to aim at being between the 2nd and 4th ranks in display networks and between 2nd and 8th on the search pages. This will translate to you being in the first position in the second search page. Use the "Position Preferences" option in AdWords to advise Google of the position you want to be in. Your bid price will be lowered and so will your position.

14. Set up Different Bids - As a way of managing your bottom line and advertising budget, consider setting different bids for different keywords. Google offers you the option of setting a standard default amount for all the keywords that appear in the same ad group. However, you can also set a different amount for certain keywords depending on their importance to your campaign. Therefore, instead of having a blanket bidding price for all your keywords, you can determine which keywords in your ad group are more important to your campaign than others. You can allocate a differential bid price to those keywords that are very important to your overall strategy. To better understand the bidding system, I highly recommend watching a Youtube video from Hal Varian, the Google Chief Economist: **Google Adwords Bidding Tutorial.**

15. Schedule Your Ads - Changing your ad position throughout the day can enhance your ads' click-through rate. This means that it is important for you to track what times your ads receive the most clicks. The Performance Reports from AdWords and Google Analytics will be your best tool in determining your most profitable hours. Another essential tool is Ad Scheduling, which allows you to tell Google when to raise your bid – and thus your position – in both the display networks and search pages. In the advance levels of

Ad Scheduling, you may determine the rate at which your bid should increase throughout the day. Note that Ad Scheduling will apply to all ad campaigns that are in the same ad group.

16. Optimize the Click-Through Rate - By optimizing your click-through rates, you can lower your pay-per-click costs. One effective way of increasing your CTR rates is by developing targeted specific keywords. Remember that targeting and staying relevant are more important than bidding highly. High bids do not guarantee high CTR, but targeted keywords do.

17. Use the Language Settings - How about speaking a different language to target a similar market? Translating your ads into different languages shows that you are keen on reaching people from all over the world. AdWords lets you translate ads into 38 languages. However, you must not compromise on anything that makes an ad effective. This includes using target specific keywords, maintaining high quality copy on all your pages and bidding for the appropriate position. As mentioned previously, it is also important to remember that automatic translation tools are never 100% accurate when converting from one language to another. It is always best to use a translator or consult a contact who is fluent in the language you are converting to. The page that users land on must be written in the customer's language, otherwise you will be generating unproductive traffic. If you are going to go international, your business must be prepared in terms of shipping products and maintaining language specific customer and sales services.

18. Use Google Alerts for Your Keywords - Using Google Alerts as a source of keywords used in your industry will keep you ahead of your competitors. The importance of keywords in developing effective AdWords campaigns cannot be overstated. For your keywords to target the right customers, they must be industry specific. Keeping up with trends in your industry is an indispensable way of knowing which words your target audience are likely to use when looking for a certain product or service. You can also go a step further and discuss trends with industry experts, who are naturally a good source of information for insider details. All these efforts are geared toward staying relevant to the evolving needs (and search behavior) of your customers.

19. Keep up with Your Quality Score - The AdWords program is cyclical and continuous, always adding, removing and reshuffling ads on the display network and on the search pages. Your ad campaign must also demonstrate continuity and currency. Testing your ads frequently is an effective way of determining the quality and value of your keywords. One way of doing this is by building two different ads using a similar keyword and seeing how they perform. The ads that are not performing well should be deleted or improved upon. In addition, keywords that cease to generate significant traffic over a period of time should be removed or improved. Continuously checking and testing your ads will help you write compelling ads and prevent you from wasting revenue on less effective ads. Google recently added a new feature in AdWords, which should save advertisers' time diagnosing issues with their keyword quality score. If you hover over the status bar of your keywords, a dialog box will appear with three new quality score indicators. These indicators are for **Expected Click-Through Rate** (CTR), **Ad Relevance** and **Landing Page Experience**, and they are rated according to Below Average, Average and Above Average.

20. Use Keyword Insertion - Relevant traffic as opposed to conversion rates is a good perspective to take. Remember that you are also looking for visibility, and not just sales. Therefore, focus on the ways in which you can generate the good kind of traffic to gain visibility. From there, you can establish your credibility with potential customers. Another advanced method of optimizing traffic is to use keyword insertion, which allows you to build a regular ad by using a large category of keywords. This way, when searchers look for a product you are offering, one of your standard advertisements will come up immediately. However, it is important that the keywords you use fit naturally with the ad copy. This will improve your quality scores and make you look professional to customers who see your ads.

21. Check the Industry Averages - Knowing when to increase your budget will give you more mileage in terms of attracting relevant traffic. Although one of the strategies of maintaining a good ROI on your ad campaign is to keep the costs low, you must determine just how low is low. One of the factors to consider is the industry average – metrics that you can get from Google Analytics. Industry averages show you how your competition is doing in terms of keyword usage, traffic and click-through rates. If the industry average rates on keyword values are low, then this could be an opportunity for you to bid higher and beat the competition. This is especially applicable if your services or products do not (yet) face stiff competition. Consider that a rock bottom low budget will disqualify your ad from appearing in all searches that are related to your ad group keyword.

Chapter 9
ADSENSE: MAXIMIZING REVENUE FROM YOUR CONTENT

AdSense is a Google web-hosted program that provides businesses (also known as publishers) the opportunity to generate revenue by placing advertisements on their websites and blogs. AdSense is a free service, and applying to the program is simple. As soon as your AdSense account is activated, you can begin showing advertisements that are useful to your targeted audience.

The AdSense program can become a significant part of your business revenue stream while allowing you to gain greater online visibility. However, this largely depends on how well you organize and manage your website to accommodate profitable ads and long-term partnerships. Here are some AdSense tips to use in your business for greater profitability.

Content Optimization - Optimize your webpage to accommodate only those ads that are compatible with your content. Optimizing your webpage for the most relevant advertisements means that only those ads that are likely to be clicked by your target audience will appear on your site. You can create content with low competition and low volume search keywords and link (via internal links or links in the sidebar) to pages on your site that have content with high CPC keywords. On high CPC keywords content pages you can place your AdSense ads. A clear strategy for webpage optimization is likely to increase the click-through rate, thereby increasing you revenue stream. To optimize your webpage, use the main keywords in both the content body and in the title. Include these keywords in the meta-tag description and in the H1 and H2 tags.

Ad Placement Optimization - One of the most fundamental areas that your AdSense campaign should focus on is how to optimize ad placements. Strategic ad placement can have a positive effect on the click-through rate. Most site users are scanners, and very few of them are readers. As you optimize your AdSense placement, focus on the areas both scanners and readers are likely to look at. A suitable section to place your best performing ads is on the top left-hand side of the site page. It is also a good idea to place advertisements in areas that have visual displays such as drawings and graphs. This way, the ads are more likely to catch the attention of the users. In addition, placing the ad within the content is an effective way of generating greater click-through rate. Overall, ensure that the AdSense placement does not distract readers who are looking for information before they can click on ads, as this can have a negative impact.

AdSense Niche Sites - Niche sites offer the greatest rewards for AdSense campaigns. Create and develop your site to target a specific niche rather than a general market. Businesses that generate the most revenue from their AdSense campaigns often cater to a specialty market. This is because ads placed in a niche site tend to have greater click-through rates and pay better, thus boosting your bottom line. Although not all niche sites generate a lot of traffic, they attract users who are looking for very specific information and products. One way to set yourself apart as a niche site in your industry is through providing high quality niche related content. High quality content will not only improve your Google rankings, but they will also earn you high paying ads.

The AdSense Referral Programs - Providing your site users with free resources will keep them on your site for longer and increase click-through rates. Google offers web publishers another source of revenue generation with their sites, through the various referral programs. These are usually free software downloads that might be of use to your site users. Every time a visitor to your site downloads any of these programs, Google will pay you. Some of these downloads include the Firefox browser with Google, Picasa, AdSense subscription and AdWords. It costs nothing to participate in these programs, so it is worth a try.

Rich Media Ads - An AdSense campaign that chooses to display image and video ads will attract more advertisers to bid for ad placement on your site. Both the image and video ads compete with text ads in a similar bidding process. An effective approach to increasing your AdSense revenue stream is to allow both text and rich media advertisements to compete for placement on your site. Google uses page-indexing technology to establish the most profitable and relevant ads to assign to your site. It is worth noting that when you choose to display video ads on your site, Google will pay you based on impressions and per click.

Ad Sizes, Colors and Fonts - The visual display of your site, and that of the ads, plays a significant role in affecting click-through rates. Optimize your site and ads for a seamless user experience. Generally, the ads that have the highest click-through rate are the large skyscraper ads, the medium rectangular ads and the leaderboard ones.

Google Custom Palette – It lets you customize the ads that appear on your sites so that they merge well with your site. Indeed, site user behavior indicates that most users typically click on blue links. What does this mean for your site? It means that you need to match your site's theme with the links and background colors of the ads on your site. This seamless merging makes the ads look like they are part of the site content.

Ad Links - While the standard ads are effective additions to your site content, it is best to use Ad Links as tools for navigation. Ad Links are links to other advertisements, and many web publishers are apprehensive when using them. However, if they are strategically placed, Ad Links can have higher click-through rates than the standard ads. For your Ad Links to perform well, consider placing them at the top of your page where the site navigational tools are placed. Be sure to match your site's background with the ad so that the ad looks like a part of the page. Because Ad Links use minimal space, it is a good idea to use them in combination with the standard ads. You just might start to see a positive change in your revenue stream.

AdSense with Google Analytics Integration - Google Analytics is an indispensable tool for monitoring a wide range of data concerning site user behavior and ad performance. Google Analytics provides various metrics that can help you in making decisions about your AdSense campaign. One of these is the "Geographies" report that shows you where most of your site users are located. It also shows which locations have the least users for your site. Through Analytics, you can determine the most profitable users (i.e., those who demonstrate the highest click-through rates). These metrics will go a long way in helping you to determine how to continue attracting traffic from the most profitable site users. The "Visualization" report is another effective analytical feature that you can use to track the performance of ads on your site over a period of time.

Your Site with AdSense for Search Integration - By integrating your site with AdSense for Search, you will allow your site users to have greater navigational power as they look through your site for information or products to meet their needs. AdSense for Search is a platform that allows users on your site to find information easily. This platform also enables users to search not just pages on your site, but also Google pages and ads. Additionally, you can customize this tool so that only web pages with ads that are relevant to your site will show up when users make their search through your site's integrated search engine.

Analyzing Queries that Promote Traffic to Your Site -
By understanding user behavior, you will be in a position to
understand how to optimize click-through rates. Analyzing
queries is a great way of finding out how users find your site
through the search engines. Google Webmaster tools
provide you with an analysis of the various search engine
queries that generated impressions and those that led to an
actual click-through. You will also get insight about the
position your site initially ranked when users used certain
queries that generated click-throughs, and those that
generated impressions. The information that you get from
this analysis will help you to optimize your site in a way that
reflects the user's queries. Naturally, this will involve
optimizing your keywords and your content accordingly.

Managing Links and Units - The number of links and ad
units that you place on your site will vary from time to time.
Do not put too many ads, as this will distract the site users.
Do not put too few, as this will sabotage your bottom line.
The best approach to take when it comes to the number of
links and units to put on your site is this: place three regular
ads for AdSense for Content, three Ad Links, and two
regular ads for AdSense for Search for each site page. If your
site is already too full with content or is too small, consider
using more Ad Links than standard AdSense ads. It is

essential that your ads appear on the pages that attract the most traffic; this may not necessarily be the first page.

Using Channels - As part of your monitoring strategy, create different channels for each ad that appears on your site. Every time you make any optimization changes, use channels to determine the effects of your optimization. Channels are the tools you use to monitor ad performance, traffic that is flowing to your site and click-through rates. You can track the performance of ads placed on different sections of your site or in different domains. Use ad channels as part of your greater ad sense strategy to determine which ads you want to remove from your site or which optimization approach you should undertake to increase the click-through rates of these ads.

Google Keyword Hints - The best keywords to use when optimizing your site are those that closely match the content on your site. Adhere to a single theme for each of your web pages. As you work to optimize your web page, you will have to invest a significant portion of your time in determining the best keywords to use for your site. Google Keywords Hints is an indispensable tool that will guide Google in determining the types of ads that will appear on your site. By submitting your keywords to Google Keyword Hint, you will essentially be taking a pro-active step in determining the type of ads that will be placed on your site. As you submit your keywords to Google Hints, it is best to limit them to three to five phrases, and to separate them with a comma.

DoubleClick - DoubleClick for Publishers is Google's ad serving platform that lets you manage your expanding AdSense business strategy. If you are gearing yourself up to venture onto more than one site, this free hosted platform will enable you to interact not just with AdSense advertiser, but also with other third party networks involved in online advertising. By joining in with Double Click for Publishers, Google will automatically choose the best paying advertisements to feature on your sites.

DoubleClick Ad Planner Publisher Center - Double Click Ad Planner Publisher Center is an interface that allows you to show potential advertisers why your site is worthwhile for their advertisements. This is especially applicable if your business is already growing at a steady rate, or if your site is attracting relevant traffic and the click-through rate is impressive. Advertisers usually use Google's Ad Planner to determine the best sites to place their ads on. Google Analytics metrics are useful in demonstrating your site's performance to potential advertisers. This strategy will gain you more visibility from the advertisers. You will also be in a position to host ads that have a higher pay-per-click cost.

Brand Protection - It may seem impossible, but the truth is that if you lack a consistent AdSense strategy, ads that feature competing products and services might appear on your site. To avoid this, you can take charge by using the "Competitive Ad filter" in AdSense, which blocks out your competition from appearing on your webpage. To block competitor's ads, enter the destination or displayed URL into the Competitive Ad filter and the tool will automatically block these ads from appearing on your site. Be careful not to click on the AdSense ads on your site in an attempt to find the URL – this is against Google policy. Instead, use the AdSense Preview tool to find an ad's URL.

Ad Color Optimization - To generate a significant amount of money with AdSense you must take into consideration the visual appeal of your webpage in relation to the advertisements. You cannot edit ads, but you can optimize your site in such a way that the ads, the content and the overall look of your site merge naturally. One approach to take is to match the border and background colors of the ad to the background color of your site. You can also match the color of the ad links with the anchor links appearing in the content of your webpage. In addition to this, you can match the font color of the ad text and the ad website with the font color of your webpage content.

Image Optimization - Although it is better to have more text than images in your websites, well-optimized images can serve as a great attraction for the types of ads that you host. Optimized images contribute to increased click-through rates. Google uses its Image Search to crawl your website to determine the number of images that you have on your site. Google Image Search will then determine how well the images on your site are optimized. Web pages with well-optimized images will rank highly in Google's page indexes, thereby attracting advertisements that have a higher pay-per-click cost. This translates to higher revenues for your business. One way to optimize your images is to include ALT text that uses the main keywords on your webpage.

AdSense Preview Tool - Installing the AdSense Preview Tool acts as an extra eye to ensure that your website is always optimized appropriately. The AdSense preview tool was launched to provide web publishers like you an opportunity to see beforehand the ads that will appear on your site. By applying this tool, you can act promptly to block or eliminate the adverts that you do not want on your site. Using this tool also allows you to test how well your site is optimized in terms of color setting and ad placement. This free tool is easy to install from your AdSense interface.

Avoid Smart Pricing - Smart pricing changes take place every week. Your AdSense strategy should be equally versatile. Smart pricing is a strategy that Google implements on a week by the week basis to change the cost-per-click on ads that appear on your page. This means that sites that do not have a high conversion rate will have the cost-per-click rates lowered. The result is that you will be earning less and less from every underperforming ad on your site. A good approach to take is to carefully use the results from your channeling reports to see which adverts are underperforming and which ones are not. When smart pricing changes every week, look at your reports to see the ads that are not generating any income and remove them from your site. Remember that one underperforming ad could affect the performance of the whole account.

Chapter 10
GOOGLE OFFERS: FEATURING ON DAILY DEALS

Google Offers is an initiative that connects businesses to customers who are looking for exciting deals on food, clothing, entertainment and much more. For businesses, this is a cost-effective way of advertising your product offering and of reaching out to as many valuable customers as possible. Through Google Offers, customers are notified through an email about the daily deals that you are offering, in a very similar way to Groupon.

As a business, you can benefit from Google Offers in several ways:

- Become more visible to the potential customers in your locality

- Use exciting deals to attract customers

- Gain visibility across Google advertisement platforms at no extra cost

- Receive quick payments without making unplanned payments

Here are some tips on how to use Google Offers for Your Business:

Creating a Deal - For you to kick-start your Google Offers campaign, you need to pick the services or products that you want to offer a discount on. You can also place limits such as the minimum amount of purchase that will qualify for the discount. Ensure that the product or service you identify for promotional purposes will be attractive to a substantial number of people; this is the best way to make profits from a deal. Also, take into consideration the profit margins of the product or service to ensure that the deal does not erode the profits that you are supposed to generate from the product/service.

Promoting and Publicizing Your Offer - Marketing your deal entails creating an ad copy that is compelling enough to attract customers to sign up for your offer. Look at this as an ad copy for your entire business and for the specific product that you are offering. Although Google will help you create marketing copy, it is essential that you personalize this copy to bring out the value that the product will offer to your targeted customers. You should also come up with a suitable time to run the offer. Like AdWords and AdSense ads, there are specific times of the day that customers will be more receptive and responsive to your offer.

Showcasing the Offer - Running your deal serves two purposes: to provide your business greater visibility and to let local customers know about the specific product or service that you are promoting. Through the Google Offers initiative, your offer will be advertised across Google ad platforms, will appear in the Google Offers pages and will be sent to local customers who subscribe to your offer. Even though customers do not make purchases on the day that your offer runs, they will have an idea that your offer exists. For customers who make a purchase, they will pay for the product or service in advance before they can receive it.

Serving Customers and Collecting Revenue - Once your deal runs, customers will use a printed or digital copy of the offer that they have purchased. To cater to your online store customers, you will use a redemption identification number to track their purchase and for them to redeem their rewards. Because there are no out-of-pocket costs for you, Google will deduct their fee once a customer has made the payments for a purchase. You can collect your revenue three days after each customer makes a purchase.

Chapter 11
MONITORING YOUR BRAND, INDUSTRY AND COMPETITORS

Google Alerts

Google Alerts is a free tool from Google that allows you to receive email notifications concerning latest news, trends and results. Google Alerts uses your queries and specifications to aggregate information from different sources on the Web, which you can access through your verified email account.

Here are some of the ways that you can use Google Alerts in your business:

Generating Leads - Staying abreast of industry trends and the people that matter in your industry is an important way of generating leads for your business. You can do this by creating alerts about clients with whom you want to do business. This way you will stay on top of what they are up to so that you can build an appropriate contact strategy.

Searching Tips:

- Using **Exact Keywords**: If you want to receive very specific alerts, you may create specific keywords by adding a (+) sign before the keyword.

- Using **Exact Phrases:** Using phrases allows Google Alerts to generate alerts that are more detailed and tailored to the key phrase. However, you can also make your search more specific by enclosing the phrase in quotation marks.

- Using **Alternating Keywords**: You can prompt Google Alerts to generate searches with alternative results by using OR in your keywords. It is important that you capitalize the letters OR. This approach lets you receive alerts with a wider scope.

- Using **Related Words or Synonyms**: You can generate alerts by using keywords that have a similar meaning to each other. You can do this by placing this sign (~) before the word.

- Searching a **Single Site**: The "Site" feature on Google Alerts allows you to track and receive notifications about a specific website. This can be a news website or a particular blog that is specifically relevant and of interest to your business.

Industry Information - Use Google Alerts to stay current with the trending news in your industry. Use specific keywords to enable Google to aggregate the most relevant news for you. The news alerts that you receive can serve as a source of information for company blog entries, for writing guest posts for sites with which you are in partnership, for client newsletters and for email campaigns. Also, by staying informed about the current trends and news in your industry, you are able to make strategic decisions concerning your products or your business model.

Competitor Tracking - Use Alerts to track what your competitors are up to. For you to remain relevant to your customers and to maintain a competitive edge you must know what your competitors are doing. To receive frequent and helpful updates about your competitors, take into consideration your keyword usage. By using keywords that are highly specific, you are more likely to receive very limited information. Unless you are looking for specific information about your competitors – say about product launches – you might want to use broader keywords. Even then, use advanced options to aggregate more relevant alerts about your competition.

Tracking Your Business - Just as you track your competitors' businesses, you should be able to track yourself, your brand and your products. By using Alerts to track your business, you will receive up-to-date information about what others are saying about your business. This also allows you to stay in touch with how effective your marketing and advertising strategies are. If you are receiving alerts about people commenting on your business or product offering, then it means that you are gaining visibility. To make the most of Alerts while tracking your business, input search keywords that will aggregate news and information about the most important aspect of your business at a given time.

Managing Your Reputation - What can you do with the information that you receive via Google News Alerts? Whilst having greater online brand visibility is a good thing for businesses, your online identity can also be compromised. When you receive alerts about your brand and some of the talking points are negative or are inappropriate comments, you need to act fast to manage your identity. "Me on the Web" is a new Google tool that you can use to manage your reputation by staying informed about what others are saying about your brand. This tool lets you reply to responses and talking points in the various social networks.

Monitoring Content Usage/Plagiarism - Maintain the integrity of your website content by using Google Alerts to track any sites and blogs that copy your content. If you have content that is frequently stolen by other publishers, you can use a part of that content or the whole of it to generate an alert. When another publisher posts this content on his or her site, you will receive alerts about this activity and you will be able to take the necessary steps to have the plagiarized content removed. The best way to track content from your website is to be very specific about what you are tracking. Using specific words that occur in your content such as a person's name or the name of a place will bring you better results in your alerts.

Track Links - Link building is an essential networking strategy for businesses with an online presence. You can use Google Alerts to track inbound links to your site, thereby discovering potential partners in your niche area. Tracking links entails getting informed about other sites that are talking about you and essentially driving traffic to your site. This provides you with the opportunity to send guest posts to those sites that your target audience is visiting. While you track inbound links to your site, you can also track links to your competitors' site to see the audience and sites that are linking to your competition and how you can get others to link to you too.

Answer Questions - A smart way to interact with your targeted audience is to be their go-to person when they need solutions that your business or product can provide. Customers go online looking for answers and solutions. They post their questions on platforms such as Yahoo Groups and expect to find an expert answer. You can use Google alerts to remain informed about the questions your target audience is asking. By answering these niche specific questions, you will begin to establish yourself as an expert. Then, follow this up with soft selling that will direct them to the solutions that your business offers.

Chapter 12
TRACKING AND MEASURING RESULTS

Google Analytics

Google Analytics is a Google hosted tool that allows you to compute the sales generated by your online business. This tool is also useful in determining the rate at which users in your site are converting to purchase your product offering. Additionally, Google Analytics offers you detailed insights into how site users are interacting with your site. With this tool you are able to determine what is working and what is not in your online business. Here are some tips for using Google Analytics in your business:

Internal Statistics - By installing a search box within your web pages, you will be able to track various site user behaviors. With an internal Google powered search box within your website, you can find out what visitors are looking for within your website, what search words they are using, what pages these words are taking them to and what pages within the web site they are visiting the most. By installing the internal search engine within your site interface, you will be in a better position to optimize your site in a way that visitors are able to easily find what they are looking for.

Configure Alerts - Alerts are a great way of finding out about traffic trends to your site and any irregularities in your website that require consideration. Analytics Intelligence generates automatic alerts accompanied by overview reports and sends them to your email inbox or through SMS. It is also possible to customize the type of alerts that you want to receive at any given time. You may choose the criteria for alerts, such as alerts about traffic trends to your site in the last two weeks. Analytics Intelligence also collects historical information about traffic trends to your site, thus allowing you to gain insights about past irregularities.

Track Links - Use Analytics to find out which links within your web site or blog are generating the highest click-through rates or most downloads. This is especially important if those links are leading to pages that might serve to convert the site users. You can do this by including a small JavaScript code on the Analytics interface to allow Google to track the performance of links in one or more web pages. If all the links that you are tracking direct the user to a similar URL, you may tag these links in a way that the Analytics tool will distinguish one from another. For example, if you are tagging three links, all of which are directed to the same URL, you can tag them as the link 1, link 2 and link 3 and feed them in as a code for Analytics to interpret their performance.

Filter Yourself - While Analytics allows you to monitor and analyze traffic to your site, it will not discriminate traffic that you or your business employees generate to the site. Of course, this is likely to give you inflated statistics about the traffic trends, unless you filter out traffic that you or your employees generate. Use your IP address and then create a filter with Analytics so that it does not take into account the traffic generated by your company or a web development company that may be continuously looking at the site for website performance monitoring.

Creating Custom Reports - Like a personal private dashboard, custom reports are the ideal tools for time saving and customizing the type of data that you and your business stakeholders need to move your business forward. Google Analytics allows you to create reports based on the type of data that you want to see and utilize in your business. It is easy to build custom reports, and you can edit, organize, save and share them with business associates and other players in your business. You can create these reports by dragging the relevant information and then dropping it into the report until it is built to meet your business needs.

Use Annotations - Use annotations to help you remember important details concerning the activities of your website. Sometimes there is so much data, too many reports and plenty of analysis to undertake, and it is easy to forget the details of these activities. Google Analytics Annotations allows you to write notes on graphs and reports, or record the different online marketing activities you have undertaken in your business, such as displaying ads. This tool also acts as a logbook that stores information about the number of visitors to your site and the conversion rates, and you can also manage records of multiple online marketing employees. When you activate the Annotations tool, it will store the information that you consider relevant for future reference, allowing you to keep up with the changing trends on your site.

Advanced Segmentation - The Advanced Segmentation tool is one of the most used and effective tools in Google Analytics. Advanced Segmentation allows you to set aside sections of your site traffic and to analyze them independently. By using this tool, you will get in-depth insight into different aspects of site traffic. You can build your own custom segments to analyze, or you can use the pre-existing Analytics segments – for example, the "Visits With Conversion" segment. Analytics offers a user-friendly segment creator that allows you to compare the performance of current segments with past data. These comparisons between the present traffic behaviors and historical ones are effective in helping you to make decisions about marketing campaigns and optimization to improve site traffic and site-user interactions.

Site Search Data - Site Search is a tool that allows you to view how often web pages are viewed. It also lets you understand the effectiveness of the landing page in keeping visitors on the site longer. From page reports that you get by using this tool, you will be able to make decisions on how to optimize not just the landing pages, but all web pages to improve the visitor experience. In addition to the page report, the Site Search Tool will generate a Site Search Usage report that provides you insights into how many visitors used the search box to look for items or information within your site and how they actually used it. To get the most from this tool it is important that you only analyze the pages that you are expecting your visitors to search and not those they are searching because they cannot find the precise information on other pages. Finally, use the "Goal Conversion" option to provide you with the visibility of the bottom line benefits of having a site search box.

Conduct In-Page Analytics - You can find the In-Page Analytics tools in the standard reporting menu under the Content Analytics section. In-Page Analytics is a tool that allows you to analyze the visual aspects of your site. It assists you in determining whether site users are finding the content (both text and rich media) that you want them to find; whether they are responding to your calls to action that may be urging them to subscribe or share an item; whether they are clicking any links, and if they are, which ones. This tool also allows you to preview your web page layout and to determine whether it is easy for your site users to navigate. You can use the Control Bar in the In-Page Analytics report interface to choose which type of data you want to view at a particular time.

Events Tracking - The event-tracking tool enables you to use a tracking code that will track and analyze the various activities of site users. The Events tracking tool allows you to view visitor activity independently from the page views tool mentioned above. The Events Tracking tool is an accurate measure of site visitor activity when compared with the in-page view tool. When you use Events Tracking you are able to find out specific activities on specific pages rather than the total of all activities undertaken in all the web pages on your site. For example, you can use the Events Tracking tool to know the number of times people are clicking on a gadget on your site, such as the RSS feed gadget or a file download. All you have to do is use a ga.js tracking code to set the parameters of the activities that you want to track.

Social Sources Reports - Social Sources reports are useful tools in determining the most relevant social platforms to focus your social networking resources on. This tool removes the guessing from social media strategies as it provides you with the precise data on what tactics are working and which ones are not working. Use this feature to determine the social platforms that are channeling the greatest traffic to your site and to understand how users to your site are flowing from the social networks to your site. This will help you to determine how to use social networks to better channel visitors to your site. To access these reports, go to the "Standard Reporting" option that is under the "Traffic Sources" Tabs, choose "Social" and then "Sources."

Social Sharing Report - Understanding how well your content is shared across the social networks is important. This will help you determine whether the content is reaching the target audience and if the audience is wide enough to generate significant traffic to your site. If you are already using the Google +1 feature for your social marketing campaign, then Analytics will generate a social sharing report that illustrates how your +1 buttons are being shared across the social networks. You may also track the sharing activities of Facebook and Twitter plug-ins on your site. To do this, you would link these plug-ins to Google Analytics and then utilize the Social Plug-ins report to see the sharing activity of these social networking plug-ins.

Activity Stream - The Activity Stream tool is a URL hosted means of tracking the interactions that your social community has away from your site. While the Social Sharing report tracks onsite sharing of content from your site, the activity stream tool tracks the re-sharing of this content. This tool lets you view which URLs visitors to your site shared, how they shared these URLs and the platform that they used to share site URLs. The activity stream tool allows you to see the type of content in your site that is interesting to your target audience. This information helps you in determining how to create and place content in a way that will engage the target audience. It will also help you make decisions on how to allocate resources in terms of online marketing and the management of your social community.

Conversion Reports - Conversion reports are useful social tracking tools that allow you to see how your social media strategy and campaign is affecting your business bottom line. By using the conversion report, you will receive information on the click-through rates and rates of conversion that resulted from social network activities, and the monetary value of these conversions. Accessing the conversion report will determine the goals that are relevant to your business, and Google Analytics will connect these goals to the ecommerce tools. This linking will generate clear and simple data on the economical effectiveness of your social marketing efforts. It will help you to determine the type of site content that encourages conversion through the social community.

Multi-Channel Funnel - The Multi-Channel Funnel is a feature that enables you to go beyond the last click that generated a sale. This tool enables you to comprehensively analyze the bigger picture of how clicks turn into conversions and conversions into actual sales. It also enables you to see the step-by-step process site visitors take to flow onto your site and the various functions that trigger these visitors to click through or to make purchases. Google Analytics tracks the various digital media on your site and analyzes how visitors interact with these channels before they convert or buy anything from your site. The Multi-Channel Funnel tool is useful in helping you plan for your digital marketing strategy and budget.

Attribution Modeling Tools - Attribution modeling tools allow you to create and track site models that you can compare against each other to determine their effectiveness. This tool works in tandem with Analytics Goals and ecommerce to track which site models will contribute positively to your bottom line. With the Attribution Modeling Tool you can easily create models, adjust them and customize them in a way that lets you see which aspects of your site generates click-throughs, sales and conversions. By creating and tracking models, you are able to have a more realistic view of how to allocate resources to different strategies, including marketing, advertisement and optimization.

Advertising Analytics - When you integrate AdWords with Analytics, you are able to gain insights into what happens when a visitor clicks through your AdWords ads. You can use this tool to determine how effective your AdWords are in terms of converting visitors and the monetary value of the advertisement strategy. You also have access to reports such as the AdWords Keywords report that allows you to see how effective the keywords you use in your ads description are. Use the AdWords Day Parts report to gain information on the time of day that your AdWords strategy performs best. Additionally, the Destination URLs report will allow you to determine when to change the web page designs or to write the ads anew. With these tools, you will have a better idea of how to attract customers through strategic advertisement placements.

Mobile Analytics - The Mobile Analytics tool enables you to measure mobile applications and visits to your website done through mobile phones. This tool allows you to understand the types of ads that are attracting site users to use your mobile applications. You will also understand whether users are more inclined to click through the ads on their phones or from their desktop. Additionally, you will know how well users are interacting with your website's mobile phone application. Overall, mobile analytics allows you to build a mobile marketing campaign that will allow visitors to interact with your site regardless of their geographical location.

Mobile Report - The Mobile Report is a useful tool that allows you to determine how effective your mobile application offerings are with your site users. Through this report, you will see the number of visitors that access your site through mobile devices, the brand of phone they are using, the service provider and the layout of your site on mobile devices. Understanding factors such as screen resolution and operating systems will allow you to design your site in a way that is accessible to users who reach your site through mobile devices. You may also use this information to determine whether a mobile site that is independent from the desktop site is economically justifiable for your business.

Using Custom Variables to Measure Application Users - The Custom Variables tool enables you to set benchmarks that will allow you to track the type of people using your site through mobile applications. With this tool, you can create custom selections by changing the Google Analytic tracking code. You may then build a custom form on your website that allows visitors to enter their professional information such as their titles. With this type of information, you are able to intimately understand not just mobile user activity, but also the type of audience that is accessing your site through their mobile devices. With this data, you are better placed to determine how to design your mobile application to enhance your visitors' experience.

Content Experiments - Google Optimizer, Google's tool allowing us to test content on your website to see its effectiveness in increasing user conversion rates is no longer available as a standalone product, but was integrated with Google Analytics. You can access it from the Content section and you can test up to 5 versions of a single page.

The initial step in Content Experiments is to choose the page that you wish to test. Although there are no fast rules regarding the order of testing pages, it is recommended that you begin testing the page that usually brings the highest return on investment to the site and to your business in general. This does not always have to be the homepage; it can also be the categories or product description page. Test a variety of content, images, calls to action and layouts to find out how effective they are in converting site visitors.

Webmasters tend to overlook copy optimization. However, it is essential to test site copy because the quality of content will affect your search engine page rankings. Additionally users who are keen on buying anything from your site are likely to comprehensively read the site copy. Through the

'Heat Map' application, Google Optimizer allows you to test the number of visitors who actually read the content on your website.

When a page brings more conversions it can be classed as a 'winner' and you can put that page live.

Google Webmaster Tool

Google Webmaster Tools is a free web-hosted service provided by Google for webmasters. As a business with an online presence, this tool allows you to monitor the indexation of your website and to make your site more visible on the search engines. Google Webmaster Tools is easy to use once your account is verified.

Here are some tips on how to use Google Webmasters Tools in your business:

Use Webmaster Tools to Show any Errors on Your Site - To ensure that site visitors get direct and easy access to your site, it is essential that you monitor any errors that may be present on your site. You can use Webmaster Tools to determine if there are any broken links to your site or if some links are channeling traffic where there is an invalid page. You may also use this tool to find out if you have blocked Google robots from crawling some of the pages on your site. Take into consideration that if you block Google robots from crawling pages on your site, it will be difficult for anyone to find these pages through the search engines.

Site Design Outlook - It is important that you design your site in a way that will allow Google robots to crawl and to index your site sufficiently. It is recommended that you create a site that has well-organized text links, preferably organized in a hierarchical order. Ensure that each link directs site users to a direct page. Use site maps that indicate the most important sections of your site. This will enable site users to find information easily as they navigate through the site. Although you may want to provide users with as much information as possible on your site pages, it is advisable not to have too many links within a single page. Overall, ensure that your site has more text based content than images; it is much easier to crawl text than images.

Technical Site Outlook - On the technical aspect, you can allow Google robots to crawl and index your site better by minimizing the use of features such as cookies, JavaScript or Flash media. Other features that may make it difficult for your site to be crawled sufficiently include session IDs.

Although these features may be helpful in monitoring site user behaviors, they may pose as a hindrance to complete site crawling and indexing. It is recommended that you monitor the performance of your site, especially the time it takes for pages to load. Use applications such as Page Speed, Webpagetest or YSlow to test your site performance. Remember that a faster loading time improves the experience of site users. By improving the technical quality of your site, you will be able to improve site performance, including loading time.

Quality Site Outlook - A quality site will go a long way toward improving your search engine page rankings. Thus, it is important that you continue to improve your site by creating site pages that are targeted towards your site visitors and not the search engines. It is advisable that the content on your site pages relates to the descriptions that are displayed in the search engines. To enhance and maintain the credibility of your site it is recommended that you avoid black hat search engine optimization techniques. These techniques include keyword stuffing, link buying and spamming. These techniques may initially work for a few days, creating the impression that they're successful, but this success will be short lived and they will ultimately lower your page rankings. A good approach to take is to provide high quality and relevant content for your site users; this way, users will find you easily through the search engines.

Using 301 Redirects - Webmaster Tools allow you to set the 301 status for your site when you move pages to a different URL from the one showing in the search engines. This ensures that users will still be directed to the page that they are looking for on your site. Setting a 301 status for your site is especially important if you do not want to incur a high bounce rate because visitors cannot find your site or the pages that they are looking for. 301-status setting is also applicable if users access your site through different URLs. It is advisable that you use Webmaster Tools to choose a URL address that will serve as the destination. Then, use the 301 status to redirect users who are accessing your site from your other URLs back to your chosen destination URL.

Indicate the Preferred Domain - If you are using multiple URLs, or if one of your domain names has expired, it is a good idea to set a URL through which users can access you. This will allow Google robots to recognize your different URLs as belonging to the same site. The preferred URL or domain name is that which you want Google to index as belonging to the pages on your site. Your preferred domain may take the form of the www or non-www; either way, remember to indicate which domain you want to be indexed as your main domain. In this way, users will find you even if you change your domain name or move pages to a different URL.

URL Geo-Targeting - Use the Webmaster Tools to inform Google about the country that you would like your site to be related with. This is especially applicable if your site targets visitors in one or more countries. By informing Google about your countries of preference, Google will be able to optimize your domain in such a way that it appears in the search results of people making queries in the target country. For example, if your product offering targets people in Ireland and South Africa, you can optimize your domain in a way that your site has a higher page ranking when users in these countries enter a query that relates to your site or the type of products that you offer. Optimizing you site for geo-targeting will not affect how your site appears in the generic search results.

Use HTML Suggestions to Amend Your Site - Through Webmaster Tools you can access reports that show you the irregularities present in your site. As Google crawls your site, it will identify problems that are keeping your site from optimal performance. Although these identified problems do not keep Google from crawling your site, it is important that you pay attention to them and amend them to improve site performance. The reports are great tools that offer you suggestions to problems such as content that does not meet the quality guidelines and as such cannot be indexed; problems with page titles and meta descriptions; or problems with ALT descriptions for images.

Canonicalization - Canonicalization is another name for selecting your preferred domain if you are using multiple domains for the same site. Canonicalization allows you to manage the appearance of your site URLs in the search engines. This technique also enables you to aggregate information such as the popularity of links and the number of site users that access your site through each URL that the site has. It is a good idea to set a canonical link for all the different pages in your site. This is particularly helpful in optimizing all the pages on a website so that search engine queries direct the searcher to a very URL specific page. This technique is helpful if your site has many pages, each of which is as important as the other one.

Author Information - Use Webmaster Tools to allow information about you to appear in the search engine results when people search for your content. To do this you will require a complete Google+ profile that you will link to your content or site. You may link your content to Google+ through a verified email address so that your address appears in the Contributor section of your Google+ pages. Ensure that the email address you use in your profile is on a similar domain to your content. Be sure that the articles you post on the given domain have a precise description indicating that you are the author of the content. From here, all the articles that you publish are searchable on the search engines and will have your authorship information accompanying them.

Creating Sitemaps - Sitemaps are a catalog of all the pages that appear in your site. Sometimes Google robots may not recognize some pages on your site, and the creation of site maps allows you to inform Google about these pages. Create and submit site maps to inform Google about various aspects of your site including rich media, textual content or software codes. Sitemap creation and submission is particularly useful for new sites that do not have too many links, or have rich media (images and video). This technique is also helpful for sites that have too many pages that are inadequately linked to each other. Site map creation ensures that all of your web pages are indexed appropriately for the search engines.

Creating Sitemaps for Different Sites - In addition to creating site maps for the pages in a single site, you may also create and submit site links for all the sites that you have. Instead of creating and submitting a site map for each site independently, you may create a single sitemap that incorporates the URLs of your various sites. Then you can save this sitemap in one location. This approach will save you time and allow you to manage and properly organize your site maps. Before incorporating site URL into a single sitemap, all these sites should be verified by Webmaster Tools.

Instant Preview - When users make queries in the search engines, Instant Preview allows them to quickly scan the content and outlook of the web pages that appear in the search results. These previews are important for users as they help the user to determine if they will click through to the websites displayed in the search results. Whether an instant preview appears alongside your search results depends on your preference; you may choose to have it appear or not. However, if you have high quality content and an impressive site layout, having an instant review activated alongside your site in the search results is a good way of inviting visitors to your site.

Schema - Unlike humans, search engines do not fully understand the precise meaning of the content and words in your web pages. For example, if the pages in your site are dedicated to discussing all things in the country of Turkey, the search engines do not always recognize this. They may bring your site into search queries that are looking for turkey, as in the bird or poultry. To enable the search engines to recognize your content very specifically, you can add tags to your site pages' HTML code. A combination of these tags is known as microdata. Schema.org is a platform shared by Google, Microsoft, Yandex and Yahoo that enables webmasters to add microdata into their site HTML. You can access Schema through your Webmaster Tools account to start adding tags to your content, thereby making this content more specific in the search engines.

IMAGE PUBLISHING BEST PRACTICES

Provide Adequate Information - When using images within your site, it is important to ensure that Google is able to crawl and index these images for search engine optimization. One way to do this is to provide as much information as you can about the images. Specifically, important information includes complete and descriptive filenames. Filenames that are descriptive are not only important for SEO purposes, but they also make it easy for users to find you and the relevant images that you have on your site.

Use ALT Text Correctly - The ALT text allows you to provide information to site users and search engines about the image and what it contains. A properly written ALT attribution allows Google to decide the most relevant images on your site to display when users submit a query as a search. In addition, some of your users and potential customers may be unable to see the images on your site because they are visually impaired, have a slow Internet connection or have screen readers. By providing detailed ALT texts, you will enable users to understand what the image contains even if they cannot see it. It is also essential that you use keywords moderately in your ALT text descriptions.

Protecting Your Images - Webmasters usually block people from using their site images without permission. This approach might protect your site from image plagiarism and deter others from using your site bandwidth. However, blocking your site in this way may limit the people who can have access to your site and you may hinder the search engines from discovering your images. A better approach is to allow users to have access to your images, but they must attribute these images to your site.

One way of doing this is to avail an HTML description that people can use to incorporate your images into their site so that they can in turn provide the appropriate attribute and backlink to your site. The Creative Commons is another international platform that you can use to protect your images whilst at the same time allowing others to access and share these images.

Optimizing User Experience - One way of making site images visible and accessible to users is to create independent pages for each image. This is particularly important if you have plenty of images, all of which are important and relevant to your targeted audience. When you create independent landing pages, be sure to adequately describe each image by providing captions, tags and informative meta descriptions. Also, consider placing images at the top of web pages to ensure that these images are visible to all users.

Using Anchor Text - It is not entirely possible for webmasters to determine how their sites will appear when they are linked to other people's sites. However, you can ensure that the anchor texts available on your site are helpful and relevant to your site users. Well-placed and descriptive anchor texts offer site users a seamless experience as they link from one page or site to another. Let your anchor texts be precise and descriptive enough to tell users where the link will lead them. It is also recommended that you place images close to relevant textual content; do not mislead site users with anchor texts that lead to pages or sites that are unrelated to the anchor text description.

Optimizing the Images - To ensure that your site images are adequately indexed for the search engines, Google requires that these images have proper dimensions. Webmaster Tools allow you to determine whether your site images have the correct dimensions, and to adjust them to the appropriate dimensions. Use Webmaster Tools to specify the dimensions of your images, including the width and height for all the images that appear in your site. Take into consideration that images with proper dimensions are likely to load faster, thereby enhancing site users' interaction with your site.

Video Content Markup - Marking up your video content entails tagging the video HTML in a way that makes the content very specific in the search engines. Video content markup allows Google to index the videos that appear on your web pages so that these videos are visible in the search engine results. You can mark up video content in the same way that you mark up textual content, using the Schema.org vocabulary database. However, Google will also consider video content that is marked up through tools such as RDFa or Facebook Share.

Video Sitemaps - Google Video Sitemaps found under "Webmaster Tools" is an effective method of informing Google about the availability of videos embedded in your site. Webmaster Video Sitemaps is especially applicable when you are using features such as Flash or JavaScript as navigational tools for your site images and videos. When users locate your videos through the search engines, these navigational features will direct users to your site for the complete video.

Chapter 13
HOW TO STAY INFORMED

As a small business owner, it is essential that you keep up to date with all the trends in your industry and in the online marketing world. Tools are constantly evolving and Google is always developing new Tools for launch. You simply cannot ignore what Google does each and every day because the way Google operates can have a significant impact on your business and your online marketing campaigns. From changes that could affect your rankings to new applications that can save your business a ton of liquidity, Google has such a massive role to play. The best way to keep track of these changes and to stay on top of the changing online environment is to follow the best and most useful Google blogs that are out there.

12 Google Blogs to Keep You up to Date

Here are the top 12 blogs that I would recommend as the most useful for you. They are the ones that I regularly review, and will be the most helpful to you on a daily basis. For additional resources I suggest checking **Google's Blog Directory** (google.com/press/blog-directory.html) as Google has 130+ blogs in 17 languages, covering news about various products, technologies and initiatives. In this directory you can also find direct links to their Google+, Facebook or Twitter accounts. The first blog recommended is the Google Official Blog that provides insights into the Google products, technology and culture.

- *Google Official Blog* - googleblog.blogspot.com

The following two are not official Google blogs, but they provide a lot of useful information. The first one is from a Google employee called Matt Cutts, who joined the company in January 2000 and is now the head of the Webspam. On his blog he provides updates on the search engine index and SEO issues. The second one is ZDnet, a website that provides the latest news on technology. They have created one section on their site called "Googling Google," dedicated to Google products and tools.

- *Matt Cutts: Gadgets, Google, and SEO* - mattcutts.com/blog
- *Googling Google: ZDNet* - zdnet.com/blog/google

The next blog is specific to small- to medium-sized business users and provides tips and tools to help grow your business.

- *Google and Your Business Blog* - googleandyourbusiness.blogspot.com

The rest of the blogs recommended here are product-specific. You should check them out if you use any of these Google products and tools:

- *Google Webmaster Central Blog* - googlewebmastercentral.blogspot.com
- *Analytics Blog* - analytics.blogspot.com
- *Google+ Blog* - googleplusblog.com
- *YouTube Blog* - youtube-global.blogspot.com
- *Blogger Buzz Blog* - buzz.blogger.com
- *Google Android Official Blog* - officialandroid.blogspot.com
- *Google Commerce Blog* - googlecommerce.blogspot.com
- *Google Drive Blog* - googledrive.blogspot.com

I would recommend that you start following these blogs today to not only keep yourself up to date on any development and learn some useful tips from industry recognized experts, but also to help you to continue to learn about the best use of all of the different Google tools.

As well as monitoring Google-related blogs, I've also listed a Google+ Page you may wish to Circle, two Google YouTube channels you may want to check out and an interesting and informative Twitter account.

1 Google+ Page to Circle

Google+ Your Business

plus.google.com/+GoogleBusiness/posts

2 Google YouTube Channels to Watch

YouTube Google Business Channel

youtube.com/user/GoogleBusiness

10 million views

66,000 subscribers

Google Analytics Channel

youtube.com/user/googleanalytics

4 million views

47,000 subscribers

One Google Twitter Account You Should Follow

Google SMB: Tools and tips for small-to medium-sized businesses

CONCLUSION

Throughout this book, I've taken you on a journey with Google tools. Starting with some of the basic tools available to you to organize your business, we have then gone through the more technical aspects of Google tools and those that will help you to drive traffic – and ultimately customers – to your business.

These tools are only my recommendations, and the ones that I personally find most effective. As with anything, you will, over time, find what works best for your business and what you're most comfortable with using. I suggest that you try everything when it comes to online marketing, and try using the vast array of Google tools available. Some will work for you, and others may not. Some may also not work initially, but it may be well worth persevering.

I hope that you have found this book to be very useful and informative, either as a novice in the world of online marketing or as an expert who's looking for guidance in the sometimes confusing world of Google tools.

Marketing your business with Google can be a daunting task if you're just starting out, but don't worry: follow my advice, make use of all the resources available to you and don't give up. We've all started at the same level at some point, and if at first you don't succeed, then try and try again. It will be well worth it as a rewarding journey for you and your business.

US: amazon.com/dp/B00851Y7PA

UK: amazon.co.uk/dp/B00851Y7PA

IT: amazon.it/dp/B00851Y7PA

ES: amazon.es/dp/B00851Y7PA

FR: amazon.fr/dp/B00851Y7PA

CA: amazon.ca/dp/B00851Y7PA

BR: amazon.com.br/dp/B00851Y7PA

Connect with the Author:

Website – www.gabrielataylor.com

Twitter – www.twitter.com/globalndigital

Pinterest – www.pinterest.com/taylorgabriela

Linkedin – www.linkedin.com/in/gabrielataylor

Facebook – www.facebook.com/globalndigital

"Google is all about getting the right information to people quickly, easily, cheaply – and for free. We serve the world – all countries, at least 100 different languages. It's a powerful service that most people probably couldn't have dreamed of 20 years ago."

Sergey Brin

"Basically, our goal is to organize the world's information and to make it universally accessible and useful."

Larry Page

"SOCIALIZE TO MONETIZE"

Social link building is an integral component of your online visibility and social marketing strategy. Inbound links from authoritative and pertinent sites indicate that your own website has quality content for your audience. Creating links makes you visible to key contacts in your niche, builds trust between you and your customers/audience and boosts your personal brand as an expert in your field. Here is how you can optimize your online visibility through social link building:

1. Creating Social Profiles

Social media sites are valuable platforms for link building at a low cost. Although the value of social links is still contentious among SEO and social media professionals, you can find effective ways to leverage the power of these networks.

There are different types of social media sites and I only listed below the ones I use on a daily basis:

- *Social Networking Sites:* Facebook, Twitter, Google+, Linkedin, Xing, Ecademy, CafeMom

- *Curation Sites*: Pinterest, Storify, Paper.li, Scoop.it

- *Social Bookmarking/Tagging:* StumbleUpon, Del.icio.us, Digg, Reddit

- *Social Publishing Sites:* Squidoo, Hubpages, Ning

- *Video Sharing Sites:* Youtube, Vimeo, Viddler

- *Photo Sharing Sites:* Flickr, Instagram, PhotoBucket

- *Blogs*: WordPress, Blogger

- *Microblogs:* Twitter, Tumblr, Posterious

- *Documents Sharing*: Scribd, SlideShare

- *Personal Broadcasting:* LiveStream, UStream, Blog Talk Radio

- *Reviews*: Yelp, Epinions, Amazon, eBay, TripAdvisor, Lonely Planet Forums, Angie's List

• *Social Q&As:* Linkedin Answers, Quora, Yahoo! Answers, Answers.com, Sprouter

• *Social Events:* Linkedin Events, EventBrite

• *Location Based Networks:* Google+ Local, Gowalla, Foursquare, Facebook Places

• *Group Buying:* Groupon, Living Social, Crowdsavings

Create a profile on all the main social networks, personalize your URL with your business name (socialnetwork.com/yourbusinessname) and then link them to your **tweetdeck.com**, **hootsuite.com**, **sproutsocial.com** or **seesmic.com** accounts. These sites will allow you to schedule and post on multiple social platforms from a single dashboard. It is also recommended that you ping the URL of a web page each time you posted new content for a faster indexing by the search engines. To do this you can use **pingler.com**.

FACEBOOK: Facebook offers a wide and active audience that provides a great opportunity for linking. Link building on Facebook entails interacting with the people who are

257

already in your network, either for reciprocal or one-way links to your site. You will be surprised at how willing your connections on Facebook are to link to your site when you simply ask them to.

Consider establishing a Fan Page for your business and then ask your friends to join the page. Post promotions, special offers and coupons, or articles related to your business or niche. This way, people will link to your site as they share this information with their connections on Facebook.

TWITTER: Twitter is also a valuable tool that allows you to connect and engage with other users. Even though the level of connection on Twitter is sometimes fleeting, you can follow and engage key contacts in your niche and from this relationship, they can mention you and link to your website.

Twitter allows you to embed your website URL in your posts and updates. This way, those who follow you can go directly to your website, learn about your business and link back to your website if it offers high quality and relevant content.

LINKEDIN: unlike Facebook and Twitter, you can greatly grow your connections on LinkedIn. You can send InMail to the people you are connected to. A paid LinkedIn account also lets you send InMail to people who are not directly connected with. InMail is a great way to reach people because it has a high opening rate. The 'InMail' simply introduces people to your business and if they like what they see, they might link back to you.

PINTEREST: the 'Popular' section on Pinterest will show you the most popular images; these are typically original and compelling. When you post unique pictures on your board, other users are more likely to repin, like and comment on them. Coupons and QR codes are valuable tools to use in attracting an audience and get repinned. This engagement goes a long way in making your brand more popular on the social site. Users can also comment on content pinned by other users as well share this content across the site and on other social networking platforms.

YOUTUBE: like other social networking sites, YouTube has an active community in which people interact, share ideas, leave comments, ask questions and share content. By commenting on other people's videos, they get to know that you exist. This is also a great opportunity to showcase your expertise and to attract people to what you have to offer. Look around for groups in your niche or those that your local customers and prospects are likely to be in. Join and interact with people in these groups and soon you will have the opportunity to introduce them to your business. Always direct viewers to your site after they watch the video. Embedding a link to your site is just the beginning of the conversion process, from viewer to potential lead. In addition, you may create an independent landing page within your site for users who visit your website from YouTube. You may use this landing page to showcase product/service offering or to capture visitors' information for list building.

GOOGLE+: leverage the effectiveness of the + 1 option. You can place this sharing button in your website, in ads and in your content too. Whenever a user +1s the content you distribute to them, they create an endorsement for your brand. The content is also shareable with others in the user's Circle. Placing the +1 button in your content will go a long way in allowing your audience to engage with your brand.

Host a hangout for your customers and those in your Circles. Leverage the power of Hangouts to have question and answer sessions with your local community and customers. You will be surprised by how much your customers appreciate getting their questions answered especially before making a purchasing decision.

Use Ripple to see how users interact with the content that you post. Ripples not only allow you to connect with Google+ influencers, but also to see how your content is shared on the platform. Visit the Ripples page to see the most influential followers for each of the posts that you send out. Influencers in your Google+ network are essential as they can help you spread the word not just about your posts but also about your brand and product offering.

TUMBLR: Blogs on other platforms such as WordPress, Blogger or within your website, tend to be longer. Tumblr audiences are less inclined to these types of traditional blogs, instead preferring to read, follow, like and reblog shorter, snappier posts. Nevertheless, this does not mean that you cannot leverage the Tumblr audience back to your post and allow them to see the type of content that you offer on your comprehensive blog. A good approach to take is to post shorter versions of your blog posts onto Tumblr and then insert a link or two that will direct users back to your comprehensive post/site. This way, readers who find your post interesting might be able to link back their own Tumblr or fuller blogs to your post.

Increase the number of people who read, follow and link to your blog by integrating your blog to your

Facebook, Twitter, LinkedIn or other social networks where you have a profile. **Twitterfeed.com** is a tool that could help you achieve this. Your blog posts will be published automatically on your chosen social networks and your readers would be able to link back to your site or blog. Also do not forget adding social buttons to each page on your site to increase the number of Likes, Shares, Pins, +1s or +Ks.

Social Meet-ups: Do not let your social link building start and end online. Attend meet ups and conferences to meet key people in your field. Remember that networking and getting the right connections is at the heart of link building. At these local conferences, you will gain insight about other people's businesses and thus the opportunities available for you. Meeting and interacting face to face with your potential partners is much more valuable than sending them an email or phoning them to inquire about a link building opportunity.

2. Submitting and Publishing Guest Posts

Guest blogging has the capacity to furnish you with high quality links, if you take the time to select your guest blogging partners. In fact compared to social networks, guest blogging may offer higher quality links. Here are some best practices for guest blog posting:

Build Your Portfolio

When you contact a blog owner or a guest blogging platform for the opportunity to post, they will want to see your content. If you are just getting started, use your blog as your portfolio. The type of content to submit is different for each guest blog platform. Pay attention to the requirements to improve the chances of your content being accepted. Overall, all authoritative guest blogs require high quality and relevant content.

Find the Best Guest Blogging Opportunities

- **MyBlogGuest.com:** it's a great site that links content creators to blog owners and journalists. It has about 28,000 users from around the world and places daily around 200 articles. It also gives you the opportunity to personalize your profile by linking it to your other social media sites such as Facebook, Twitter, Lindkedin, StumbleUpon, Google Plus and Pinterest. They offer three levels of service to choose from.

- **Guestblogit.com**: it's a guest blog market place where you can submit monthly one article for free. Then publishers will pick it up and publish it on their sites. You can also subscribe to their paid version where you will be paying $20 per month for 5 articles submissions and many other extras that you can find listed on their site.

- **Google:** Use the Google search engine to find relevant guest posts in your niche. Simply search for various keywords (with quotes) such as 'write for us', 'guest post', 'guest blog', 'guest blog submission', 'guest post by', 'accepting guest posts' or 'guest post guidelines', preferably accompanied by a niche term.

- **Twitter:** Use the Twitter search engine to find guest blogging opportunities posted on Twitter. Use a variation of the keywords used in your Google search.

- **Check websites in your niche:** Use tools such as **Open Site Explorer** to look at the back links that the websites in your niche receive. This is will tell you about the guest blogging sites that the blog/website owners participate in.

- **Blogs:** Look out for blogs that include the author bio and website URL at the beginning of the content. Blogs that will add the author bio and URL within the post as well as those providing a link to a website or social network profiles.

For more ideas on where to submit your content, I suggest checking two great Internet resources:

- *100 sites to submit guest posts* - bit.ly/ZUEevG
- *500 places to syndicate your content* - bit.ly/ducmAM

What to Look for in a Site that Accepts Guest Blogs

- **Page Rank:** Use tool such as **SEOquake** or **SEO Site Tools** to find out how the site ranks on Google search engines.

- **Domain Authority:** Use a tool such as **SEOmozToolbar** for Chrome and Firefox to determine the site's domain authority.

- **Subscribers:** These are site followers from Twitter, Facebook, Pinterest, Google+, YouTube and other social networking sites as well as those who have subscribed to the site RSS feed.

- **Traffic:** Use **Alexa Ranking** to determine the amount of traffic the blog attracts. A lower number on Alexa indicates higher traffic. **Google Ad Planner** can also give you insights into the number of visitors to the site.

3. Running Promotional Contests

Hosting online competitions can help you attract links from various domains, key contacts (such as press publications) and authority sites.

Basic contests and promotions entail asking users to visit your website, to enter their details, answer a question and then finally determining the winner. The type of prize that you give away largely depends on you profit margins and bottom line.

By partnering with others in your industry to host the contest or promotion, you will not only gain publicity but also backlinks. In making their audience aware of the contest or promotion, your partners will mention you on their sites, thereby driving free traffic to your own site. You may also endorse other people's contests or promotions by offering additional prizes, in exchange for a link.

Make use of competition lists to list your contest/promotion. These sites will definitely link back to your site as they refer participants to your landing pages. Although your competition might take a few days before being listed, it is still worthwhile to leverage these sites. Good competition sites to look at are **Loquax.co.uk**, **ThePrizeFinder.com** and **CompetitionWinner.com.au**.

Send your competition to loyal Twitter followers, bloggers or any key contact you may know and who will not mind covering the contest or promotion. This will help you gain publicity, generate traffic and a few good links to your website.

Leverage the shareable nature of videos to make your contest/promotion more visible. Use platforms such as YouTube and Flickr to publish your videos and include a link to your website. Allow people to share the video across other social networking sites such as Facebook, Tumblr, and Pinterest and within YouTube too. The more people share and mention your promotional video, the more backlinks you are likely to generate.

Link up with local publications including newspapers and magazines with an online presence. These publications are usually willing to mention your contest or promotion in their website, thereby offering you an authoritative back link.

4. Submitting Articles to Article Directories

Article submission to authoritative directories and listings is an excellent technique to drive targeted and free traffic to your blog or website. Some of the most known article directories are: ehow.com, squidoo.com, hubpages.com, ezinearticles.com, examiner.com, technorati.com, gather.com and ideamarketers.com. Article directories have different requirements for the content they accept on their listing. High quality and well-written articles are generally accepted. Pay attention to the keyword requirements. Avoid stuffing your article with keywords and instead strategically place them in the article title, meta description and article body. Use a tool such as **Textalyzer** to check your keyword density, which should be between two to five percent.

Here are some factors to consider when looking for suitable directories and listings for link building:

It is built for human use: The main aim of a directory should not be to solely optimize your rankings. Check to see if the site owner is especially active on blogs, forums and social communities. Such a site is most likely engineered for pure SEO purposes and not for human use. It is unlikely that this site will provide you a high quality link.

Selective: Sites that offer high quality links are typically hard to get in. Such directories have editors who review submitted articles before publishing them on the site. Examples of selective directories are **Nature.com**, **Forbes Best of the Web** and **About.com**.

High ranking: The sites that offer valuable links are those that rank well for the search terms that they target. A site that cannot rank well for its own title tags will not provide you the visibility that your articles deserve.

Associated with a trusted domain: Directories and listings that have their own domain may not always offer high quality links. However, those that are part of successful, well-known and trusted sites are more likely to provide you with high quality back links.

If you enjoyed this section of "Socialize to Monetize", you can grab your copy here:

US: amazon.com/dp/B008JGPPMK

UK: amazon.co.uk/dp/B008JGPPMK

IT: amazon.it/dp/B008JGPPMK

ES: amazon.es/dp/B008JGPPMK

FR: amazon.fr/dp/B008JGPPMK

CA: amazon.ca/dp/B008JGPPMK

BR: amazon.com.br/dp/B008JGPPMK

If you liked this book you may also be interested in purchasing my "Give Your Marketing a Digital Edge" series

GIVE YOUR MARKETING A DIGITAL EDGE - VOL. 1 (6-Book Bundle) – www.amzn.to/10XUmzX

Budget Marketing: How to Start & Market an Online Business with Little or Zero Marketing Budget: why pay for online tools when there are fantastic free ones available that will help your business for absolutely nothing?

Plan, Create, Optimize, Distribute: Your Strategic Roadmap to Content Marketing Success: by mastering content marketing, you can connect with customers on a personal level, build a relationship, call your audience to action, and provide a platform for customer feedback.

Targeting Your Market: Marketing Across Generations, Cultures & Gender: marketing by demographics can be as simple as not advertising baby diapers on a site aimed at Baby Boomers. But the truth is there's a lot more to know if you want to maximize business success and avoid blunders.

Mobilize to Monetize: The Fast Track to Effective Mobile Marketing: when you use mobile technology to promote a brand and its products and services anytime, from anywhere, you can target your messages based on information you already have and engage your customers directly.

Advertising in a Digital Age: Best Practices for AdWords and Social Media Advertising: learn how to use online advertising to reach more people, interact with your community, collect feedback and monitor results in real-time, adjust your advertising quickly, and target and retarget your messages for relevancy all on a tiny budget.

Globalize to Monetize: Taking Your Online Business to New Markets: marketing globally requires cultural understanding and overcoming barriers of language and culture are crucial to successfully market globally.

GIVE YOUR MARKETING A DIGITAL EDGE - VOL. 2 (4-Book Bundle) – www.amzn.to/10XUmzX

Google Best Practices: How to Build and Market Your Business with Google: YouTube, Google+, Google+ Local, Google News, Google SEO, AdWords, AdSense, etc.: this book tells you how you can make money using everything Google has to offer.

Socialize to Monetize: How To Run Effective Social Media Campaigns across the Top 25 Social Networking Sites: by mastering content marketing, you can connect with customers on a personal level, build a relationship, call your audience to action, and provide a platform for customer feedback.

Pinterest Marketing - The Ultimate Guide: if your customers are on Pinterest, you need to be there too! Leverage the power of visual marketing with one of the best tools ever invented to increase sales for your business.

Tumblr for Business - The Ultimate Guide: learn how to use Tumblr to showcase your brand to a worldwide audience, create social buzz, and take your business to the next level.

WANT TO GET PUBLISHED?

It is often said that everyone has at least one book in them in their lifetime. Ever wanted to write and publish a digital or paper book but don't know where to start?

That's where Global & Digital (www.globalndigital.com) come in. We publish both fiction and non-fiction and we will edit and format your manuscript, design your cover, convert for publishing and distribute your book for you and also run your promotional campaigns. We can even arrange for an audio book recording or translate your book and cover into a number of different languages. We provide assisted self-publishing services for independent authors allowing you to take your book and get it published easily and affordably in a wide range of different formats. We are not a traditional publishing house, but instead provide authors with support and expertise. As such, all the profits you make from future sales of your books will be yours.

We have many years of experience in Digital Marketing, Writing and Publishing allowing us to offer our unique range of professional services. **Check all our services at www.globalndigital.com and let us take your work to market!**

www.ingramcontent.com/pod-product-compliance
Lightning Source LLC
Chambersburg PA
CBHW051211170526
45166CB00005B/1841